Abstraction in
Avant-Garde Films

Studies in Cinema, No. 32

Diane M. Kirkpatrick, Series Editor

Professor, History of Art
The University of Michigan

Other Titles in This Series

No. 27 *Ben Hecht: Hollywood Screenwriter*   Jeffrey Brown Martin

No. 28 *American Film Acting: The
        Stanislavski Heritage*   Richard A. Blum

No. 29 *Hollywood and the Profession of
        Authorship: 1928-1940*   Richard Fine

No. 30 *The Political Language of Film and
        the Avant-Garde*   Dana B. Polan

No. 31 *Subversive Pleasures: The Reflexive
        Dimension of Literature and Cinema*   Robert Stam

No. 33 *The Filmology Movement and Film
        Study in France*   Edward Lowry

No. 34 *The Free Years of the Italian Film
        Industry: 1930-1935*   Elaine Mancini

No. 35 *On the Kino Front: The Evolution of
        Soviet Cinema in the 1920s*   Denise J. Youngblood

No. 36 *Hitchcock and World War II*   Sam P. Simone

Abstraction in
Avant-Garde Films

by
Maureen Cheryn Turim
Assistant Professor
Department of Cinema
State University of New York at Binghamton

UMI RESEARCH PRESS
Ann Arbor, Michigan

ALBRIGHT COLLEGE LIBRARY

Produced and distributed by
UMI Research Press
an imprint of
University Microfilms International
A Xerox Information Resources Company
Ann Arbor, Michigan 48106

Library of Congress Cataloging in Publication Data

Turim, Maureen Cheryn, 1951-
  Abstraction in avant-garde films.

  (Studies in cinema ; no. 32)
  Bibliography: p.
  Includes index.
  1. Moving-picture plays—History and criticism.
2. Abstraction. 3. Experimental films—History and
criticism. I. Title. II. Series.

PN1995.T79 1985   791.43'75   84-28100
ISBN 0-8357-1629-5 (alk. paper)

Contents

List of Illustrations   *vii*

1   Introduction: Tracing the Rupture of the Avant-Garde   *1*

2   Beyond Reading: Image, Imagination, Aesthetic Economies at
    Play   *7*

3   Sound: Beyond Distinctions Between Music, Noise and Speech, A New
    Process, A New Ordering   *29*

4   Gradual Transformations and Subtle Changes   *51*

5   Visual Dynamics, Referential Tensions and Conceptual Film   *73*

6   Flickering Light, Pulsing Traces   *93*

7   Scanning Landscapes and Collapsing Architectures: Shattering the
    Grounding of the Subject/Eye   *107*

Plates   *133*

Notes   *151*

Selected Bibliography   *159*

Index   *163*

Illustrations

Following page 132

1. Larry Gottheim, *Blues*

2. Larry Gottheim, *Fog Line*

3. Larry Gottheim, *Barn Rushes*

4. Barry Gerson, *Luminous Zone*

5. Barry Gerson, *Translucent Appearances*

6. Paul Sharits, frames from *T,O,U,C,H,I,N,G*

7. Michael Snow, *Wavelength*

8. Michael Snow, ⬅———➡

9. Michael Snow, camera apparatus for *La Region Centrale*

10. Ernie Gehr, *Wait*

11. Ernie Gehr, *Wait*

12. Ernie Gehr, *Serene Velocity*

13. Hollis Frampton, *Winter Solstice (Solariumagelani)*

14. Hollis Frampton, *Autumnal Equinox (Solariumagelani)*

15. Hollis Frampton, *Zorns Lemma*

16. Hollis Frampton, *Magellan: At the Gates of Death*

17. Larry Gottheim, *Horizons*

18. Larry Gottheim, *Mouches Volantes*

1

Introduction: Tracing the Rupture of the Avant-Garde

My purpose in undertaking a theoretical investigation of the cinematic avant-garde stems from my own fascination with and attraction to these films. My goal was to develop theories which help to explain their functioning. But equally, I choose them as an object of study because, by the very radicality of their functioning, they suggest the necessity for revising and expanding film theory, and the implications extend to theories of figuration, representation and the processes of signification in general.

The films included in this study can be seen as continuing a work of change, expansion, deviation, and transgression of the fundamental assumptions culturally and historically assigned to filmic expression. Continuing, because other avant-garde film movements (i.e., the surrealists, impressionists, and abstract film of the Twenties in France and Germany, or the earlier American works, including Maya Deren, Marie Menkin, Stan Brakhage) had in their own ways undertaken this project.

Before further definition of the films that will be the subject of this book, some general discussion of film history from a theoretical point of view will be helpful. Cinema, unlike spoken or written language, can, in a certain sense, be understood as having "begun" in our recent past, if not our immediate lifetimes. But there can be no philosophical assurance tied to the immediate history of this beginning, for a number of reasons. Derrida has shown the necessity of deconstructing the search for an origin of speech and writing as inseparable from a critique of philosophy; in proposing the notion of the trace and of a nonlinear history of traces as a new way of approaching a history of writing, he offers a method of escaping the ontological arguments surrounding both the origin and essence of cinema.[1]

We should also remember that cinema had antecedents (in terms of various of its characteristics) in many other artistic and communicative apparati before it. The apparatus was put to uses that were historically determined, which grew out of the prevailing visual and artistic ideologies operating at the turn of the century. Each film, then, becomes a trace of what cinema could be; if the "development" of filmic expression has seemed to take certain directions, a linear striving for the accomplishment of a depiction of "reality," this history needs to be analyzed according to its ideological and economic determinants. Cinema as a concept and a mechanical process never necessitated a single or uniform usage or functioning. In fact, historians and theorists of film have only begun to analyze this history in ideological terms. By concentrating on uniform principles informing a dominant cinematic expression, the classic Hollywood film, they have tended to overlook both the differences within this model and the existence of other cinemas alongside that which they termed "dominant." They have failed to recognize the simplification of the problem inherent in the postulation of this imaginary model.

   To look at cinema through the history of its traces is to develop a concept of "filmic writing" as a scene of writing in the largest sense of this phrase, as a space of inscription. The avant-garde films I will be discussing can be defined as challenging a certain normative filmic practice, a type of coded inscription which has been analyzed as the classic narrative film and the modernist narrative alternative. As will become clear from my discussion of these models, I am not asserting that they are anything more than theoretical models of coding processes traced in films. The codes are culturally determined as well, shared by filmmakers and film viewers, although some of the codes are those which develop complex analogies to perception. By exploring the coding processes which have been established in other cinematic usages, we can come to understand avant-garde filmmaking as comparable to what Julia Kristeva has called "a revolution in poetic language," as a restructuration of filmic expression.[2]

   Metz has proposed understanding classic film as a "class of textual systems."[3] While each film remains singular, the films of this class share particular codes as well as an ordering pattern, a process of mixture of codes which can be seen as characteristic.

   Narrative codes in this class of classical film can be compared to those of what Barthes calls the "readerly text," in speaking of the traditional novel.[4] Narration operates as a vector, a linear projection from beginning to end and is irreversible. The temporal unfolding of the film is also the temporal inscription of an enigma which establishes nearly at the beginning our desire for its answer; the questions are multiplied, the central enigma is kept alive until disclosure coincides with the ending, as "truth" is revealed. Within this narrative hermeneutic, characters perform series of actions which form the basic segmental units of the film; these series are "closed" in that there is a logic of mutual implication between the first action in the series and the last, often relations of causality as in couplings like entrance/exit, question/response, seek/find. These segmental units depend on clear temporal and spatial relationships, but this organization of space and time can vary. It is in analyzing the principles of this syntagmatic organization that theorists have met great difficulties. The model proposed by Noel Burch in the first chapter of *Theory of Film Practice* remains little more than a chart of possible commutations according to rather limited factors of that ordering.[5] Metz's "Syntagmatic Analysis of the Image Track," charts a variety of possible spatial and temporal organizational patterns but is hindered in its exclusion of sound as a factor which helps to determine these units.[6] Further difficulties become evident when one tries to analyze any given film by these methods, since the criteria of analysis are not so much located in relationships among visual signifiers in the image as in signifieds in the narrative. Paradoxically, it is the temporal and spatial signification of the syntagmas which is the goal of the analytical effort. What emerges from both these efforts, however, is that there is a pattern of constraint in the spatial and temporal organization of classic films. The specificity of any given film is always an articulation of difference limited by the imperatives of the weaving of narrative codes in a traditional narrative text.

In speaking of the smaller scale articulations of the classical film, the specifics of sound and image registration, composition and montage, one can generalize only with caution, as the highest degree of variation is found here. Perhaps the most subltle way to uncover the constraints governing the classical pattern at this level of articulation is to see that the freedom with which a classical film can introduce silences, excessive sound, offscreen sound, camera movement, blurred images, changes of focus, or color or camera angle (i.e., any obtrusive structural void, excess, or more generally, any obtrusive mark of the cinematographic apparatus), is conditioned by the location, at least eventually, of an explanative cause, use or purpose of that effect. There are, however, exceptions to this generalization, even some that are quite conventional. The most obvious is the intrusion of nondiegetic music, music lacking any source within the space of the story. However, nondiegetic music is conventionally employed in a manner isomorphic with the mood or tone of the diegetic moment with which it coincides.

Another way of generalizing about the small scale articulations between sound and image is to say that they are woven together with the spatial, temporal and narrative codes to place the viewer of the film in what has been called a "sutured discourse."[7] This initially means that the camera angles and their variation from shot to shot are selected so as to provide an imaginary entrance for the viewer to a scene. As a process, suture is complicated by a complex movement between "omniscient" or "objective" point-of-view and "subjectivity," the coincidence of the spectator's sight line with that of a character. However, we can say that in the spectrum of possibilities within which the classic film operates, there is a standard of placement. An imaginary participation is encouraged that generates an illusion of a flowing, unified vision from shot to shot, scene to scene. The spectrum includes a privileged vision (the omniscient view which appears to focus on the most noteworthy framing at any particular moment) or a vision of motivated restriction, for which the narrative codes have supplied significant reasons.

The modernist film is the site of a rupture, a negation of the classical textual ordering. The codes of the classic film are partially broken (distorted, refracted) or certain codes are maintained while others are totally dismissed or deconstructed. The modernist text is a break, but often, also, a holding action, a renewal, a revitalization, a defamiliarization of narrative filmic experience. Robert Bresson serves as an excellent example of a modernist filmmaker in that his films break many codes of classic construction (primarily the codes which establish continuity and what was described above as a "sutured" flowing vision and narration), opting rather for fragmentation of vision using spatial and temporal ellipses.[8] Yet Bresson stringently maintains other codes (visual and auditory analogy, narrative hermeneutics). Ultimately what is affected is the viewer's position; the modernist film in its most determined application of these principles, re-positions the viewer to the narration. It creates a critical distance on narrative involvement and spectacle which the classic film continually struggles to maintain.

The terms "classical" and "modernist" must be understood as relative concepts. Classic codes are not absolutely standardized or adhered to in the degree of standardization which a generalized analysis tends to construct. Any given film which may be termed classical may contain degrees of rupture, and similarly, modernist films vary greatly in the degree as well as the type (location) of the break.

The above qualification must further be seen as inherent in the definition of textual systems of a film as presented by Metz; he defines textual systems "as the systematic displacement of codes in a single text."[9] If each film displaces codes, then each film can find its way into a norm only by an overall similarity in its manner of displacement. Once one really begins a close analysis of individual classic films, there is the discovery, in the midst of the confirming patterns, of the continual play of differences which embed the modernist tendencies at the heart of the tradition. I will come back to this notion of the deconstructive reading of classical films which discovers a play of difference and of force operating of a level beneath the representational surface. For now it is more important to this effort at distinction and definition to concentrate on typical patterns of representation.

This brings us to the definition of the avant-garde, which can now be seen as a more extreme application of the principles of rupture, deviation, and change than are evidenced by the modernist cinema. The hermeneutics of narrative form which dominate the classical narrative film's structure and are most often retained in some changed (inverted, open-ended, elliptical, contradicted) form in modernist film are nearly always absent from the works of the current avant-garde. This is not to say that no narrative remains, but rather that narrative is now a discourse without the developmental logic and/or fullness of pluricodic expression associated with the traditional notion of narrative. Narrative becomes fragmented actions, a series of events whose representation is undercut, submitted to an obtrusive conceptual frame that can range from restriction or limitation to excessive expansion. In the early avant-garde movements of the Twenties on through the Fifties, the novelistic tradition of narrative logic was sometimes replaced by another narrative logic. Thus impressionism is ordered by a stream of consciousness, and surrealism's startling representations and associations followed a certain conception of dream logic and the unconscious. Increasingly these logical orders have lost their avant-garde edge, being adapted into classical and particularly modernist films. The recent avant-garde, then, stands in a different position with respect to representation, and its role in building a logic of narration. Narrative of sorts may finally emerge, but its representation is the site of a continual activity of questioning.

We can pause here to underline this last point as a crucial proposition in the definition of the avant-garde film (sound and image, what Metz would call signifying matter) is significantly altered so that the processes of signification tied to cultural tradition, a set of expectations, are opened up. By "opened up" I mean on one hand made less automatic, opened to questioning, reflection, but also, given more possible paths to trace out. This reworking of representation, which sometimes takes on the violence of a destructive attack, simultaneously gives more play to processes other than representation that are also generated by the inscription of image and sound. The avant-garde directs the viewer's attention to this play of what I will call "force" and will discuss at length in the next chapter.

With this two part definition established, the restructuration of the processes of signification and the increased attention to the play of force, I have yet to set up criteria for the selection of specific films from the avant-garde to serve as my examples as I pursue the development of an analysis and a theory. The films I have chosen to include in this book are not to be understood as the limits of avant-garde filmmaking in recent years, or even necessarily the best or most interesting. They are some of the most well known, which was a choice I made out of consideration for the reader. Most of the filmmakers are American, but Michael Snow is Canadian, Dore O. and Werner Nekes are German and Peter Kubelka is Austrian. At the time I originally was gathering examples of films that raised the theoretical issues I wished to discuss, fewer women than men were working at this sort of filmic abstraction and this book does not address this issue directly any more than it examines other sociological factors surrounding the films. The focus is on the films signifying practice and the issue of libidinal economy. Although I attempt detailed descriptions to support my analyses, it is clear that no verbal description could be adequate and that every description is already an analysis of the film. Therefore I have selected films that have been more widely seen. Further I have not included many types of films normally considered avant-garde and included in the existing anthologies. The films of anarchist and personal poetics and computer generated, kinoscoped films are notably absent from this discussion; I do not mean to imply that they are not avant-garde, that the films I discuss are the only avant-garde films in existence. Avant-gardes differ greatly in their signifying and expressive practice and the limits of my study to certain types of filmic operations necessitated the concentration on certain types of films. I have in fact no theoretical interest in defining the limits of avant-garde filmmaking practices as if it were some type of closed genre. On the contrary it is a growing category and a practice which thrives on the expansion of its principles and techniques rather than the reiteration of standardized formulas.

I have not yet considered how we can speak of processes of signification of cinema's component matters, sound and image. It is necessary to explore this question to provide a more precise notion of how representation in extra-linguistic expression can be discussed and analyzed, so that the specific problem of speaking of the undercutting and transformation of representation in the avant-garde can be explored in greater depth. The next two chapters, then, will explore these questions. The four remaining chapters are devoted to the analysis of the functioning of various types of avant-garde films according to these theoretical principles of image and sound expression in film.

The organization of the last four chapters is not the parallel logic of categorization, but a loose structure chosen to explore various questions. Chapters 4 and 6 are each concerned with films that share a principle of image construction (gradual transformation over a duration in the case of 4, flicker in 6). Chapter 5 explores disjunctive uses of expressive qualities of the image and then compares this to efforts to reduce evocative image qualities in favor of a filmmaking practice that approaches conceptual art. Chapter 7 reverses the organizational modes of the other chapters by grouping films according to their representational concerns (landscape and architecture) in an attempt to show how the films, in undercutting the coded tradition of spatial representation, affect subject placement. The attention to the play of force in relation to signifying processes will be the concern of all the chapters, so that the divisions into specific topics can be seen as indicating how this activity is differently evoked in a variety of avant-garde films.

2

Beyond Reading: Image, Imagination, Aesthetic Economies at Play

Analyzing the image is no simple task; a suitable methodology needs to be sought in the theoretical investigation of both iconic representation and imaginary investment. The diverse forms of avant-garde film imagery evoke the entire history of representation and abstraction in the graphic arts. In order to analyze these films one must bring to them a critical awareness of the debate on how we see, understand and respond to the image.

Although preceded by various theories of iconography and iconology to which it is indebted, semiotic theory represents a major advance in image theory by opening visual images to a rigorous analysis of their processes of signification.

Certainly the work of Roland Barthes on the photographic image played an important role in establishing the field and initiating the methodology of this semiotic inquiry. The questions he raised in his article, "Rhetoric of the Image,"[1] remain fundamental for anyone concerned with the signification processes of cinema: "How does meaning enter the image? Where does meaning end? What is there beyond?"

Unfortunately, Barthes's own conclusions in this same article retained a notion very similar to formulations on the realism of the photographic image proposed by André Bazin; Barthes still wants to speak of a "denoted image" of an "absolutely analogic nature" which "constitutes a message without a code." Unlike other image production (drawing, painting, etc.) Barthes contends that the photograph does not obey rules of transformation in the production of the discontinuous signs:

The coded nature of the drawing appears on three levels: firstly to reproduce an object or a scene by means of a drawing necessarily implies a set of rule-governed transpositions; there is no natural state of the pictorial copy and the codes of transposition are historical (notably those which concern perspective). Secondly, the drawing operation (i.e., its coding) necessitates straightaway a certain division between the significant and the insignificant; the drawing doesn't reproduce everything, and often even very little, without ceasing at the same time to be a strong message, whereas the photograph, even if it can choose its subject, its frame and its angle, cannot intervene in the interior of the object (except by trickery)....In the photo—at least at the level of the literal message—the relationship of signifieds to signifiers is not one of "transformation" but of "recording" and the absence of a code clearly reinforces the myth of the "natural" photograph; the scene is there, captured mechanically, but not humanly (the mechanical is here the guarantee of objectivity).[2]

The postulation of this denoted level of the photographic image does not negate the interest of the rest of the article. Barthes's analysis develops a methodology for reading the image by examining units of meaning in their production of ideology, units he labels as "semes" and "ideologemes." Furthermore, even if, upon examination of the counter-arguments, we agree that it is wrong to speak of a purely denoted level of the photographic image, we can still acknowledge that the appearance of such a level is a dominant cultural (ideological) assumption and see Barthes as one of the most recent and articulate perpetrators of that assumption. Insofar as this is true, he performed a service in noting the role this assumption in turn plays in naturalizing the symbolic message:

A pseudo-truth substitutes itself surreptitiously for the simple validity of the openly semantic systems: the absence of a code deintellectualizes the message because it appears to establish the signs of culture in nature. This is without doubt a historically important paradox: the more technology develops the diffusion of information (and especially of images), the more it provides the means of disguising the constructed meaning under the appearance of the given meaning.[3]

The corrective to Barthes's argument comes from two sources, based on two separate sets of principles. Umberto Eco's argument against the concept of the lack of a code in the photographic image stems from his rigorous examination of what constitutes a code. He argues first against what he calls the "dogma of double articulation," that is, the assumption that visual and audial (extra-linguistic) expressions must be measured by the standards of codicity operative in verbal expression. Secondly, he argues for the recognition of a systemized iconic code which serves as a base for more analytic codes (iconographic, stylistic, rhetorical) but which is also dependent on other codes (perceptive, recognitive, transmissional) for its articulation. Eco asserts that "iconic signs reproduce certain conditions of perception of the object, but after having selected them according to codes of recognition and after having noted them according to graphic conventions; as a result, an arbitrarily given sign denotes an apperception arbitrarily reduced to a simplified representation."[4] Eco maintains that the principle of selective representation constituting analogic iconic signs is equally valid as a characterization of photography as it is of drawing.

One problem in Eco's formulation is that instead of limiting his assertation to "representation is coded," he tends to speak of all aspects of the image as coded. He posits such codes as the "tonal code" which includes the inscription of force and tension and the "codes of the unconscious" which supposedly structure codifications which are capable of permitting identifications or projections and of stimulating given reactions.[5] These formulations suggest that Eco's theory of the subject constitutes that body primarily as a cipher of the text; he apparently refuses to recognize that when one speaks of the force of the unconscious and the primary processes, one is considering those aspects which escape representation in any directly decodable manner. Eco follows these formulations with his own disclaimer, allowing that some of what he has been calling "codes" are best seen as "connotative subcodes" or "simple repertoires" which are not signs structured as oppositions, but are articulated as oppositions through the laws of an underlying code.

This remains schematic, easily adaptable to the diagrammatic tendencies of Eco wherein the viewers' relationship to art can be charted as information transfer between two machines or communication transfer between two speaking individuals. As will become clear by the end of this chapter, one of my major concerns is how one can speak of the interaction of the artistic expression in the object with the intersubjective activity of the viewer. The complexity of this question is avoided by handling this problem exclusively in terms of coding and decoding. It is possible, however, to divorce Eco's notions of codified selection in representation from his extension of codification to areas beyond representation. We can then still value his critique of the notion of the photographic image as a "message without a code."

Metz embraced this concept of analogy as coded and suggested in his article, "Au-delà de l'analogie, l'image,"[6] that analogy should be understood as quantitatively and qualitatively varying in different types of visual images, including different types of photographic images. He suggests that semiotic analysis must analyze the codes that comprise analogy, and also those which are added to analogy, which pass through representation.

Jean-Louis Baudry added to the semiotic notion of the coded image an important ideological critique of cinema's technical operations of coding in his article, "Ideological Effects of the Cinematic Apparatus." Baudry makes the argument that the camera-projection apparatus is the site of the very processes of transformation which Barthes had denied to the photographic and cinematic image:

Central in the process of production of the film, the camera—an assembly of optical and mechanical instrumentation—carries out a certain mode of inscription characterized by making, by the recording of differences of light intensity (and of wavelength for color) and of differences between frames. Fabricated on the model of the *camera obscura*, it permits the construction of an image analogous to the perspective projections developed in the Italian Renaissance.[7]

Baudry goes on to argue that the monocular, perspectival image produced by the camera is "based on the principle of a fixed point, by reference to which the visualized objects are organized," and the perspective image thus specifies the position the viewing subject must occupy.[8] He calls this position "the space of an ideal vision" capable of fulfilling "the idealist conception of the fullness and homogeneity of being," and thus speaks of the camera as a mechanism working to create the viewer as "transcendental subject":

> And if the eye which moves is no longer fettered by a body, by the laws of matter and time, if there are no more assignable limits to its displacement—conditions fulfilled by the possibilities of shooting and of film—the world will not only be constituted by this eye but for it. . . . There is both fantasmatization of an objective reality (images, sounds, colors) and of an objective reality which, limiting its powers of constraint, seems to augment the possibilities and powers of the subject.[9]

What I find exciting about Baudry's theory is that it provides for a discussion of both the formal codes of the image and the positioning of the viewing subject in relation to the specular act, seeing these two areas in a relationship of mutual production. The image loses its naturalization, the spectator is brought from "illusionary absence" into his/her interaction with the image.[10]

Since Baudry's work has brought us to a comparison of the photographic image and the image of Renaissance painting, it is useful to examine how semiotics elaborated a model reading the Renaissance image. I will examine the model of reading an image proposed by Jean-Louis Schefer, and then show how, in analyzing other Renaissance images, Michel Serres suggests that such a methodology, while it accurately accounts for certain operations of the image, is limited. I will show how the theories of Schefer (partially) and Serres (more thoroughly) suggest that the image, even the analogic image of a representational order, contains operations and functions which are not subsumed under the processes of signification. Barthes had already hinted at this other functioning in his question, "what is there beyond meaning?" and later in his essay "The Third Meaning" comes to posit this quality as "excess."[11]

In his book, *Scénographie d'un Tableau*, Schefer takes as his central object of investigation a painting entitled *Une Partie d'échecs*, by Paris Bordone (1500-1571).[12] Schefer speaks of reading an image as traveling through the space of the image to discern various zones of meaning, configurations which exist in complex structural oppositions to one another. He will call the traversal of these zones "reading" the sequences of the painting. Space becomes intelligible due to constraints, of which perspective plays a primary role. When one reaches the limits of these constraints, the horizon line, the concave space of vision provides closure to the image; but in the painting which Schefer chooses for his analysis, the radical separation of the two chess players in the foreground looking at the spectator, reverses the transversal and directs the gaze outward. Schefer analyzes the chess players' positions, particularly the hand of the one who manipulates a pawn and is centered in the foreground, as referring to the code of placement. Through metonymy and analogy, the hand-held pawn functions as what Schefer calls "autonyme," the subject which names itself. The depicted figure becomes a discourse on the manipulation of placement in representation. I will return to this problem of placement in representation in reference to the work of Foucault in chapter 7.

Opposition amongst the various zones (analogies and *antynomies*) creates what Schefer terms the "lexias of the text." Here he is employing the same terminology as Roland Barthes used in his analysis of Balzac's short story "Sarrazine" in *S/Z*. In so doing, he is implying that a painting has units of narrative meaning comparable to the short fragments Barthes isolated and commented on in his study of literature. Thus Schefer will want to speak of both the image, what the viewer sees, and the text within the image, what develops as the image is read (its sequence explored for the oppositions which produce its lexias). The system of the painting is the articulation of these lexias within the image:

> ... one attains the structure of a painting through a commutative operation, in an analytical system that we have defined as that of the lexia. The image and the text are in a rapport of incessant implication; the rapport that connects them is never that of commentary: the text is the structural determination of the image. Their rapport is defined as a system. [13]

What seems most useful in Schefer's analysis is the structuring role assigned spatialization in organizing the image material into patterns of articulation which in some sense can be compared with syntagmas of a discourse. Although he also develops the idea of the reversibility and multiplicity of these syntagmas, this idea is introduced after much effort has been invested in building the ordered patterns by which the analyst reads the painting. Does the use of such terms as "syntagma," "paradigme," "lexia," and "text" subtly efface the problem posed by pictorial circulation which a simple acknowledgment of that reversibility cannot rectify? In what ways are the constraints and rules of a literary text being imposed on the image? The continual efforts at grouping, listing, naming, ordering and directing, which are basic to Schefer's methodology, his very metaphor of reading the image, perhaps force us to conceive of the image with a linguistic and literary temporality and mode of articulation.

Schefer comes closest to breaking out of this structuralist literary heritage in his brief reference to Julia Kristeva's notion of paragrammatic space. For even though Kristeva's theories are primarily built from literary analysis, her semiotic analysis is continually thought of as translinguistic, and her aim is to differentiate poetic language, especially modernistic poetic language, from ordinary discourse. The discussion of some key concepts in Kristeva's semiotic analysis will be useful in proposing some refinements possible in Schefer's approach to the image.

Kristeva is, above all, interested in the productivity of the text rather than a static notion of its finished structure. Her view of the text as a site of processes of production allows her to break away from an analysis which concentrates on a fixed system of signs linked, in turn, to equally fixed significations. Her aim is to render dynamic the notion of textual functioning.

Kristeva introduces the term "*signifiance*" to refer to the process of germination or engendering occurring within what she will call the "other scene" of the text or the "geno-text."[14] The geno-text is defined in opposition to the pheno-text: the pheno-text is the surface of the text which functions for communication, while the geno-text is a volume which Kristeva speaks of existing vertically to the horizontal development of the pheno-text. There is a sense, though, in which the geno-text and the process of *signifiance* are what both precede and exceed the verbalization of the text (i.e., the signifying chain or pheno-text). As such the geno-text is in some ways comparable to the unconscious, although it is not in any way to be mistaken for the specific unconscious of the writer or painter. It is rather a surrounding force which is not represented in the text, but enters into the engendering of the representation. To further explain this surrounding force that she calls the process of *signifiance*, Kristeva will speak of gestures. She considers gestures at first literally, as the movements and tones which accompany and color an articulation, without being analyzable as independent signifiers. She denies that they have a role of mere redundancy and points to other cultures and other semiotic practices such as music, where gesture has greater prominence and more independence. She then gives gesture a specific meaning in textual analysis which she calls the "anaphoric function": "Before and after the voice and the graphic sign there is the anaphor: the gesture which indicates, inscribing relations and eliminating entities."[15] The anaphor is seen as a relational function, itself empty, which opens and extends the text and thus serves as an indicator of the other-scene or geno-text. Because it is evidenced in the pheno-text as repetitions and differences, the theory of anaphoric functions seems close to Derrida's notion of *écriture*, which Kristeva briefly acknowledges.

Closely tied to the anaphoric function is the notion of paragrammatic space. This term designates the different order of the poetic text as compared to language and ordinary discourse, emphasizing the redistributive functions of poetic language. Redistribution, a constant displacement of the two axes of language (syntagmatic and paradigmatic) results in generating a space which resists translation since it is tied to a tension of negation. One way this can operate is that the intertextual functioning of a text (a Kristevian term indicating a reference in one text to another text, or a cultural or historical fact) is submitted to negation either partially or totally. There is also the possibility of a symmetrical negation, meaning that the same logic operates in both cases, but the paragrammatic functioning results in a transformation of the meaning from the reference text. Kristeva gives examples of each type of negation possible in the textual paragram in references by Lautréamont in *Poésies* to Pascal and La Rochefoucauld.[16] However, paragrammatic space need not be intertextual: it can operate within the same poem through repetitions and slight variations which generate new meanings. Here Kristeva gives the example of Baudelaire's "*Harmonie du Soir.*" In her analyses of Mallarmé and Sollers, Kristeva shows how the modernist poet extends the work of paragrammatic space. The spatialization of writing as a graphic construction gives added physicality to the redistribution of placement.

How do these theories apply to visual representation? In the case of the visual image, one can easily transfer the concept of paragrammatic space from repetition and variation of words to that of lines, color, figures. Placement and the construction of space is more clearly and easily seen operating in painting or the photographic image than in the literary text. The anaphoric function and process of *signifiance* gain perhaps even more prominence in visual images; they become important theoretical tools that allow us to see a traditional inability to speak directly about a painting's "meaning" or its mode of functioning in a new light. This recalcitrance to apply a spoken or written analysis can be seen as reflecting an understanding that the processes of *signifiance* are often extremely evident as a central focus of specular attention even in the most representational, narrative mode of painting. One is led to speak of color, texture and forms with adjectives, which refer to their force, the tensions and contrasts they generate, without necessarily feeding these observations into a global meaning of the painting. The development of a theory which explains and expands this tendency into an analysis of how a text builds a relationship to the viewing subject, or to use a psychoanalytical term, "constitutes the subject," is a relatively new critical undertaking. When Schefer points to Kristeva, it appears as a gesture which leads us away from the structural semiotic heritage evidenced in much of what he has previously said about the image and the meanings articulated in it.

It seems as if the question has become not just, "how does meaning enter an image?" but how can we, in language, speak of the generation and circulation of meaning and force within the image? How can we prevent our verbal discourse, marked by a structural logic, a necessary order of prosaic articulation, from performing a deformation disguised as "pure description"?

Isn't the metaphor "reading the image" really a cover for an act, which in taking the place of spatialized vision, supplies its own rigidity and limitations? The difference between an ideogram and an image is too often lost under that cover.

Given these questions which linger after this discussion of Schefer's analysis, it becomes useful to contrast this analysis to that of Michel Serres in his *Esthetiques Sur Carpaccio*.[17] Serres refuses Schefer's critical discipline in favor of a loose speculation, yet many of his propositions are similar. He chooses as the object of his analysis the works of Carpaccio, (1465-1526), which use perspectival and architectural codes in ways comparable to the painting which Schefer chose to study. Serres's analysis concerns the construction of meaning in space:

> The painter escapes all stoning, all squandering through discourse. For him it suffices to place meaning in space. And morphology is a semantics.
> This is general. And reveals why this painting, a painting, is a source of a torrent of words. Meaning, in the semantic sense, is position in a qualified space, in or on a particular one of the thousands and thousands of qualified spaces, it is site, orientation, proximity, limit, and the pulsating complex of relations which assign them. It is, to take an example, the relationship of this closed, fixed space where a particular body erects itself as a statue and hurls a vector toward that open space absent from the painting. There is nothing which does not reduce to space, to a particular space and the complex tracings running through it. Space teems with meaning and the poor linearity of discourse spends itself to cash in on this fortune.[18]

Serres's own discourse is always circular, always a returning. This turns the meaning he is investigating in painting into an investigation of meaning in general. His philosophical ground is submitted to the image:

> I begin to grasp what meaning is all about. It is site, position, proximity, relatedness, folding and so forth. And plunges thereby toward the individuated. Toward specific difference. It is position through the exchange of positions, proximity through the transport of proximities, the channel through the sheaf of ramifications, the knot through the bifurcations, the place and the inheritance, the exodus and the flight....[19]

Shortly after this effort at a comparison of the morphology of narration, the preaching of meaning with the Bible, Serres will return to the painting, but now to establish it as a much more problematic space than the one Schefer acknowledges. His discovery of circulation, repetition, variation and negation becomes the discovery of his own writing. He will not fix a linear reading for analytical purposes; he will enter into process, expose it in his own writing activity:

> Let us come back to the morphologies, to the two syntagmas of the painting. The geodesics of the great wall and the path envelop the directive vectors, close them and obstruct them. These forms are contradictory between themselves. Like the lance and the great wall, the

door as access to light and the black hole, the ark and the rear wall, the invaginations of the footpath and the double dihedral of the group, the narrow passage of listening and the imperceptible angle of intersection. One traces meanings and one covers them over; one places arrows, the other puts them in a quiver; closes directions, obstructs meanings. Then, yes, both fill space with lines and with curves, they are pure syntagmas, but speak, but are the meaning of the scene: that towards which everything converges is closed. The space of unabated contradiction, both vector and edge, is identical to the space of abolished meaning.[20]

Serres provides an extremely radical response to the semiotic analysis of the image. He will begin with an attention to structure (which he will call morphology) that will serve to establish isomorphisms: the articulation of relations within the spatial constructs of the painting which parallel each other and reiterate a discourse. For example, his analysis of Carpaccio's painting of St. George struggling against the dragon branches out to consider how St. George, as a figure in the painting and as a myth in the culture, unites the three god forces of holy father, warrior and producer. However, Serres will go further to deconstruct the isomorphisms, questioning the symbols on which they are composed.

A good example of Serres's deconstruction of his own analytical discourse, his willingness to submit everything to recombination, is the essay on the "Two Courtesans." Serres first "reads" the painting:

The series of symbols form a linear phrase, is a first narrative. It is the historiogram of the two women. And the painting is their story. Or if one prefers, the vital drama of only one from youth to maturity, or better still, the essential time of femininity in general.[21]

Then he departs from the constraint of this order, pushing towards circulation:

I no longer consider the two linear series, placed in parallel, where each element is put in relation which each element of the neighboring series in a biunivocal manner. I no longer consider a phrase and its meaning, nor the contract of decoding. The method is foreclosed, it is fatally drowned. I consider all objects. I obtain something like a space and its tabulation.[22]

Serres thus reaches the point where the multiple and the relation are posed as such. Still he must question the nature of that "reaching." Is his initial reading a necessary precondition, parallel to the notion of denotation, which provides the support for new considerations, new meanings, parallel to connotations? If this were all he were saying, his theory would not represent any significant departure from Barthes or Schefer. Serres's contribution is to suggest repeatedly how the painting contains all the operations that he as analyst and theorist formulates: he grants to the object, the painting, an activity of recombination which is contemporaneous and copresent with what the analyst might for convenience posit as a first meaning. He emphasizes the existence of the abstract within classical form, and refuses to linearize the activity of the image:

> My theoretical effort cancels itself and the painting mocks me. It exists, already formed, cultural productions ahead of my discourse.... Freudian theory and my algebraic construction are only versions, recent ones if you will, of these formations already there,... The entire method is in the painting: linear phrases, the one to one relations, the tabulation of crossed series, the schema of isomorphisms.[23]

Spatial configuration for Serres inscribes the recombination of symbols and signs. The image is understood as an active space which compares to Kristeva's notion of paragrammatic space discussed earlier. These similarities are not coincidental; Kristeva cites Serres's writing on Liebniz in developing the concepts of *signifiance* and they converge on a redefinition of semiotics as the analysis of the process of the production of meaning rather than the simpler model of the coding and decoding of meanings. The notions of intertextual and intratextual circulation have expanded the focus of contemporary semiotics. It has become increasingly interested in historicizing its analysis of permutations in signifying orders as well.

This shifting of critical concerns is pertinent to the analysis of the image in avant-garde films, for these images, like those of contemporary art, operate differently than the images of the Renaissance tradition upon which the analyses of Schefer and Serres are based. How does the avant-garde image function in relation to this history of representation? How does it suggest different answers to the questions of how meaning enters the image, where meaning ends and what is there beyond?

Whereas the Renaissance image contained a readable order of representation, even though it contained more, even though relations could be drawn in such a way as to reverse this order, the image as it has developed since the Renaissance is increasingly concerned with critiquing that order of representation. Jean-François Lyotard has taken as his project the analysis of this "new plastic order," this "major mutation of desire" as he has termed it. Lyotard provides an answer to the question of what exists "beyond meaning" in the image by developing a new theory of the application of psychoanalytic theory to art.

In his essay, "Freud selon Cézanne,"[24] Lyotard is critical of Freud's own essays on applied psychoanalysis and art, which he claims think of the pictorial object solely according to "the function of hallucinatory representation and of of decoy." Pictorial analysis for Freud is analogous to dream analysis, the figuring out of a system of representation that contains clues of that which cannot be directly represented. Lyotard holds that Cezanne's artistic expression, contemporaneous with Freud's own writing, was investigating this very act of representation.

The value that Lyotard places on this refusal by a painting to continue the tradition of transferring a message through representation grows out of the importance he places on another Freudian concept, that of a libidinal economy. This concept describes the interaction of drives, forces and affects within the psychical apparatus. Memory traces of ideas have quantities of energy attached to them, but in the unconscious, some of this energy is in a free state. The need to reduce the overall quantity of energy is considered as the causal factor in all the transformation processes in which the psyche engages. The source of the energy is both internal (the force exerted by instincts, physical agencies) and external (excitement, stimulus of objects, ideas).

Lyotard emphasizes the notion of a libidinal economy as a flow of force and affects within a human body, between bodies, and between bodies and objects. His use of the concept contains within it a specific interpretation of the Freudian concepts of primary and secondary processes. Lyotard insists on the creative possibilities of the mobility of investments in the unconscious; primary processes are seen as continuous, atemporal, a flow of unbound energy. Displacement and condensation are considered the characteristic operations of this free energy, whereas the other operations Freud spoke of as the operations of dream-work (the taking into account of figurability and secondary elaboration) are seen as mixed procedures in which "the exigencies of desire and those of censure are respected together."[25]

The "figural" and "expression" are Lyotard's terms for the traces within the secondary processes (within representation) of the activities of the primary processes:

> Expression is the presence in the secondary processes, in discourse, of the operations belonging to the unconscious. This introduction always consists of the formation of a figure, ... this figure comes from an "other scene" than that of the scene of language, the pictorial or sculptural scene where it is produced; that which it expresses is not present in the work as its immediate signification.[26]

There is a similarity in these concepts to Kristeva's notion of a geno-text which marks the pheno-text in the form of anaphors and paragrammatisms. In developing a theory of an aesthetic economy, a play of tensions in the artwork, Lyotard is not so much concerned with explaining the genesis of art as he is in explaining its affective force on the viewer or listener. The intensities of the transformations and metamorphoses produced within and upon the constituent matter of the art object are transferred to the subject. This process differs in art which has a high degree of secondarization, (works of art in the representational tradition), and those in which this tradition is disfigured. Once disfiguration takes place, the traces of energy are more directly exhibited, in what Lyotard calls the "reversal of the unconscious" and the "plastic possible."[27] Perception of the image is exposure to energy. Lyotard uses the word "force" to refer to the art object's manifestations of energy intensities, which can take various specific forms, but share the potential to enter into and affect the libidinal economy of the subject.

I must pause at this point to make a crucial distinction between Lyotard's theories of libidinal and aesthetic economies and the Gestalt school of aesthetics as exemplified by Rudolf Arnheim, particularly since the same words, "force" and "expression" are fundamental to both schools of thought, though each uses the terms to refer to extremely different concepts.

First it is important to see the investment the Gestalt school places in the physiological and conscious (experimentally verifiable) aspects of perception. From this empirical data, the Gestalt school establishes a principle of isomorphism in which psychological patterns of the alteration in the brain are postulated as producing given psychological responses. Thus "force" is meant quite literally as a physiological response to stimuli. "Expression" is the parallel psychological response to the configurations perceived, a response which is determined by the experience of the subject with nature and human expressive behavior, e.g., "warm" colors, "whole" circles.

Force, for Lyotard, as I explained earlier, is drawn from the energetic theory of Freud. The physiological energy registered by the viewer or listener as an electrochemical response only constitutes force in so far as it enters into an affective play with various levels of the psyche, or more precisely, with the entire libidinal economy of the subject. Lyotard is fascinated by the physical energy circulating within the subject, connecting the body and mind (see the essay, "Le dent, la paume")[28] but what he means by "the inscription of force" in an object (including an art object) is the potential for psychic activity which the interaction with this object could stimulate. He will emphasize the object giving play to the operations which Freud associates with the primary processes. In the art object, the presence of these processes in the secondary elaboration, in artistic form, is what Lyotard terms "expression." His use of expression has nothing to do with a supposed link between human emotions and their "abstraction" as simple objects, colors and patterns, as it does in Gestalt theory. The terminological differences begin to suggest a far more fundamental conflict. While I believe that Gestalt theory has made a contribution to the analysis of certain visual forms, it is dangerously misleading in its efforts to "colonize" perception as conforming to a Gestalt model, ignoring the very factors an aesthetic/libidinal economy can raise. The argument against Gestalt theory on this ground has been formulated by Anton Ehrenzweig,[29] and I will summarize it, amending it with a response to the counterarguments put forward by Gestalt theorists.

Ehrenzweig takes to task Gestalt theory's emphasis on the perception of figures against a ground, which assumes: (1) that at the moment that a given figure forms the Gestalt that the ground no longer has psychological resonance;

(2) that figure and ground, while they can exchange places in perceptual forms cannot simultaneously both register; and (3) that certain shapes and patterns form a "good" Gestalt. The first two assumptions ignore the question of unconscious perception, which becomes particularly active in what Ehrenzweig calls Gestalt-free modern art, art which involves a direct appeal to a diffuse, undifferentiated vision, a "child-like" vision. Even in the most traditional art, though, this undifferentiated vision (also termed "scanning" by Ehrenzweig) affects our view of the whole. Ehrenzweig claims this explains why artists are taught to pay such attention to background shapes, colors and textures. As concerns the third assumption, that of a "good" Gestalt, Ehrenzweig points out that the introduction of this valorization of harmony, balance and unity retains all the loaded assumptions of an old aestheticism that much of contemporary art attacks.

The argument against Ehrenzweig suggests that unconscious perception is purely hypothetical.[30] Such an argument ignores the strength of Ehrenzweig's exposition of how unconscious, undifferentiated vision in childhood becomes dominated by differentiation, a process also remarked upon by Gestalt theory as "inculturation." Ehrenzweig believes that this childhood vision is retained as a scanning power that is the basis of a syncretic vision (dedifferentiation) particularly valuable to the scientist and artist, to creative thinking. Another counterargument claims that Arnheim's theories are not consistently dependent on Gestalt principles. Without reviewing in detail all of Arnheim's writings on art, one can point to his assumption of balance as an ideal in *Art and Visual Perception*, his antiverbal espousing of experience in *Visual Thinking* and his suggestion that expression (as he defines it) is the highest priority of art in both these works, as well as in an essay called "The Gestalt Theory of Expression" in *Towards a Psychology of Art*.[31] The same constructs are evident in Arnheim's *Film*,[32] where his appreciation of film techniques and the formal constituent properties of film parallel his explanations of color, space, form and movement in art. Nowhere is he concerned with how these properties enter into a process, a functioning which then can be analyzed as provoking both force and signification. The terminal point remains his notion of "expression." These analytical constructs, whether or not they encompass the totality of his works, remain in contradiction to what I consider an extremely productive view of the functioning of art in both Ehrenzweig and Lyotard.

So the theories of Ehrenzweig and Lyotard not only remain distinct from Gestalt theory, they allow for an analysis of psychoanalytical functioning of art. Still, a problem posed earlier by Serres's acknowledgement that the classic at least partially remains: how *distinct* is this new order, if the classic bears the abstract within it and representation itself undergoes historical mutations?

Lyotard takes on this question in various ways. In speaking of Cezanne's work, he compares each of Cezanne's four periods to other constructions of pictorial space, i.e., antique painting, Roman primitives, baroque art and Far Eastern water colors. In this instance one is left wondering in what sense then Cezanne's order is really "new" or, to put it differently, does Cezanne's work, like the Far Eastern scrolls to which it is compared, simply organize space into a "different" representation?

Elsewhere Lyotard considers precisely this problem by suggesting that indeed one can consider, in fact should consider, the figural as more important in art than representation, and this in all types of pictorial organization:

> It could well be that in all the representational examples including the "primitive," the classic and the baroque, the important aspect is not the ordered, the synthesis, the beautiful whole, the thing lost or rendered, the accomplishment of a unifying Eros, but rather distortion, the separation, the exteriority to all form.[33]

This leads him to wonder if the modern does not continue this "representation-disfiguration," keeping the "window-mirror" role of the canvas intact:

> In the Demoiselles d'Avignon ... and any nude of Bouguereau, the separation is perhaps no more, as Gombrich has shown, than that of a flat window and a deformed glass, cubism being certainly academicism undone, but both remain, together, representation.[34]

The answer for Lyotard is that the analysis of contemporary art cannot stop at the point at which it recognizes the apparent attack on representation or the reworking of regulatory codes. A positive theory must be formed that can place an importance on the act of production and inscription. The undoing of a given code of representation is a means not an end, a means of bringing forth a process of energy flow. The theory of the avant-garde has, above all, to understand force, dynamics, change, and to valorize the exhibition of process. It can then show how a multitude of new operations, new uses of technology and materials, opens the image as a field of play, a realm of reworking.

Energy which was contained in traditional forms can be released for either sharper or more subtle expressivity; the breaking of habitual norms allows for a broader spectrum of energetic experience. Yet the avant-garde is directly threatened by a danger which traditional art has more easily reconciled within its very system of tradition. Avant-garde art fails to fulfill its project when it merely reiterates certain formulas. The stylish reproduction of known patterns will not suffice for art whose project is to expose the dynamics of flux and process. Repetition or stasis can both play an important part in the dynamic process, creating a new awareness of minimal and subtle variation, as well as the cumulative effects of reiteration and duration, but the standardization and regulation of patterns in a balanced form remains antithetical to this dynamic theory.

In approaching the avant-garde I have come to believe that it is necessary to employ the semiotic notion of a coded image that is in some ways comparable to a discourse and to poetic language in order to investigate how the image in these films functions. I find that the images vary greatly in respect to their similarity or break with the kind of signifying practice that Baudry, Schefer and Serres have analyzed. But this semiotic path, alone, cannot acount for certain of the films, particularly the more abstract imagery, or images which are the "lack" of imagery, as in the flicker films, the abstract animation, and the reshot film stock of Ernie Gehr's *Axiomatic Granularity*. Further, to speak of codes of signification to the exclusion of the inscription of force and the engendering of affects by any of these films (and perhaps *any* film) is to exclude an area of filmic, imagistic functioning which severely limits one's analysis to certain levels of articulation. In actuality these levels are never mutually exclusive; any attempt to talk exclusively about one level alone is bound to distort the theory of the object's functioning.

Jacques Derrida has launched perhaps the most eloquent argument on the limitations the "structuralist system and method" in literary criticism, an argument to which those employing a semiotic analysis of film should listen. In his essay, "Force and Signification,"[35] Derrida writes:

> As we live in the midst of a structuralist fecundity it is too early to beat our dream to death. One must imagine what it *could signify*. It will be interpreted, tomorrow, perhaps, as a detente, if not a lapse, in the attention played to force which is the tension of force itself. Form fascinates when one no longer has the force to understand the force contained in it. That is to say, to create.

I am not trying to perform a superficial reconciliation between two theories, semiotics and libidinal economy, which despite certain overlaps are self-avowedly antagonistic. The antagonism is, in part due to the different approach semiotics has taken in applying psychoanalysis to film. Semiotics has primarily focused on the imaginary investment in the impression of reality invoked by the Hollywood film, and is based on Lacan's analysis of the mirror stage and Freud's work on fetishism. Both Metz and Baudry have made substantial contributions to this theoretical elaboration.[36] Since the avant-garde film image is placed in a tension between representation and disfiguration it often plays with or against the mechanisms of the impression of reality. The analysis of the "imaginary signifier," as Metz has termed it, has applicability to the analysis of certain avant-garde images as well; I will discuss in chapter 4 how certain films rework these mechanisms and then in chapter 7 examine how this imaginary placement is evoked and dislocated in avant-garde films treating architecture and landscape.

But the tension between semiotics and the theory of an aesthetic/libidinal economy is due to the fact that the former analyzes the process of the production of meaning and the latter the meaning of processes which are not necessarily "productive." I would like to conserve the tension as part of my own theory and analysis. Part of what I have learned about the films I am considering is that they are enmeshed in a tension, a struggle, between the generation of force and the articulation of meanings. The theory and analysis of the avant-garde film has to create itself within this conflict, to be a flexible, creative act, willing to move back and forth without adhering to dogmas.

So far in this discussion of the theory of the image, I have not considered those properties of the cinematic image which differ from painting, photography and other still images: the various kinds of movement (within the image, of the camera, of the lens), the various kinds of temporal inscription, the articulation between images, the specifics of an image created out of projected/reflected light in terms of black and white as well as color qualities, the rhythms resulting from the combinations of these factors. It is within the close discussion of films that the specificity of these properties will be examined. I will show how these elements are used in the avant-garde project of transforming the cinematic image.

To amplify how the general theoretical questions I've raised concerning the image, as well as those from chapter 1 concerning the differences of the avant-garde from traditional filmic narration and form in film, are brought together in the viewing of a film, I would like to close this chapter with a discussion of a very short, stunningly simple film by Hollis Frampton entitled *Lemon*.

Let me begin, then, a critical experiment with *Lemon*. I will try to avoid limiting the evocative force of the abstract qualities of the images; instead I will mark how these traces of light and color, line and form can generate effects which flow through multiple representations occurring within the duration of the "same" image, but which also overflow each of the representations, undoing representation as a frame.

A remark on the function of the critic of avant-garde films: to trace signifying processes and the economy of force the writer is led to suggest meanings, to record in words preliminary and pivotal stages of processes which should not be taken as closed (for the viewer) around this set of possible significations. My suggestions, in analyzing *Lemon* will not exhaust or match all viewings of the film; rather, as a set of significations and transformational moments they correspond to traces in the film and serve to expose this type of active response, its imaginative functioning. They do not replace the film viewing or complete it, but are only an element of a theory of the film's functioning.

Lemon is seven and one-half minutes of light, movement and silence. During its projection, *Lemon* confronts us as an image-object; we as subjects watch it. Its affect is for a time our libidinal economy. We are amused, bored, or seduced, and then the film ends.

What happens when the film ends? What happens when we begin to speak (or write) about it? To speak, silently or audibly, about what we have just watched, what we have just experienced with our bodies?

When we begin to speak about the film, we tell stories about it. Presumably they are not the film's stories, for *Lemon* lacks the structures and codes we associate with narrative film. The stories we tell about *Lemon* are our stories of our relationship to the image, and in our stories we trace our history.

The first story I wish to tell about *Lemon* is the story of light. This story begins with two bright highlights of white light against a yellow surface, outlined and defined by an edge on the right side of this surface, an edge forming a curved shape from which a point protrudes. This edge defines, in turn, a black background. The left side has no such defined border—it is an indefinite nebulous space, a fading. The brightness and expanse of the lit area gradually increases so that the crescent and point become the right side of an oval, the opposite end of which, the left crescent edge, is somewhat shaded, a shading which creates the impression of a lumpy surface. The light wanes from the lower left edge in a diagonal upwards as a shadow appears under the point. The highlight moves up across the yellow shape. The waning continues until all that remains is a crescent of light on the right, the reversal of the earlier shadowed crescent on the left. The very edge of the crescent and the pointed protrusion are the only parts which are lit, appearing as a translucent glow. The yellow-orange is now nearly absent—all that is left is the crescent, thin and white against black. Then the top part of the crescent edge ceases to be lit so that only the lower half of the crescent up through the point is lit. Then the image fades to black.

A blue back light appears, beginning to define the lower right corner curved area. The back light increases until it defines the silhouette of the curved shape with a protrusion on the right. The blue light turns into a yellow light. The dedication and credits end the film's verbal silence, and then the light is no more.

This was the story of light—it engenders and is engendered by movement. The light moves, its movements become stories. The reflection of light in the image is the trace of its journey. Light moving through frames of celluloid, frames of celluloid moving through light. The story of light is the story of registration and projection as well as of the transformation of the object/figure and the film image.

From the story of light and movement to the story of objects and fragments—for seven minutes we watched light and movement, first reflected over a surface and then transferred to celluloid and then projected as an image. But during the time of the film projection another story occurs, the story of an indistinct shape, becoming round, full, becoming a body, becoming an oval curved body, which we all call a lemon. As this body emerges as a unity, we can assign it a name, and it is at this moment of near wholeness that the image falls into equivalence with the word. The image is at the height of its *trompe l'oeil*; like a finely brushed and lacquered seventeenth-century Dutch still life, the image radiates the illusion of the corporeal presence of the object and its volume. Consider this speculation by Jacques Lacan on the trompe l'oeil:

> What seduces us and satisfies us in the tromp l'oeil? When are we captivated by it and when does it give us jubilation? At the moment when, by a simple displacement of our gaze, we can perceive that the representation does not move with it and it is only a trompe l'oeil. Because it appears at that moment as other than what it had given itself as, or rather, it gives itself now as being this other thing. The painting is not the rival of appearance, but rivals with that which Plato designates as beyond appearance, as being the idea. It is not because the painting is this appearance which says that it is what gives itself as appearance that Plato fights against painting as an activity which rivals his own.[37]

The displacement of our eye which deconstructs the image as being the representation beyond appearance is accomplished in *Lemon* not by our eye actually moving, but rather by the light moving and the film continuing so that the wholeness, this modeling of a flat surface into apparently three dimensions through light perspective, is only a fleeting instance. The wholeness appears just long enough to cover with its sanctity the fragments that compose it.

To cover with narrative, with unity, with complete, "full" representation, with the smooth flow of an image track, is an act which has been analyzed as a process of concealment fundamental to the functioning of classic film. But to say that unity, smoothness, and narrativity serves as a cover, is to say, as Thierry Kuntzel has pointed out, that film is split into two films.[38] One is projected under normal viewing conditions and is "read" under the terms of its representation (spontaneously by viewer, structurally and semiotically by its analysts) and the "other film," which does not offer itself up to readability, to being deciphered.

The other film is hidden, embedded either within the narrative representation[39] (i.e., repetitions, condensations, transformations, displacements of represented elements) or it is embedded within the smooth continuity of the image flow[40] (elements recognizable only when each frame of the film is stopped, which become "invisible" under the conditions of normal projection). The other film is the space where force operates, evidenced as traces which evoke fantasy investment from the viewing subject, as Kuntzel explains in his article, "Le Défilement":

> The text as a series of frames is not offered to be read in a manner parallel to the film in motion, but the fantastic elements are traceable in, under, beyond, through (the right word is hard to find) the projected film.[41]

Kuntzel gives this trace a name, "*l'émouvoir*," meaning that which moves, but also that which rouses affects, a term with a multiplicity of meanings which suitably characterizes the shimmering, flickering of traces through and throughout meanings, outside of the sign systems which distinguish representation. Again we have returned to a concept very like Kristeva's "*signifiance*" and Lyotard's "expression" and "figural space."

Lemon's covering itself with representation and the covering process Kuntzel has described in the classic Hollywood film and the animated cartoon is the same in that they share the structure of the split I have described between the film which is seen, deciphered, and that which is experienced in hiding. There is an important difference, however—the film which is "seen" in *Lemon* is so close to a joke, so far-fetched as the limits of senseless representation, reinforced by an insistent apparent stasis, that this "seen" film invites us to explore its fleeting traces, to fulfill our desire for stories. Its fascination for us is our teasing quest for meaning; it invites us to repeated viewings just when we, having decided we have been seeing nothing, discover we have been seeing too much.

So within this film about a lemon and a trompe l'oeil representation is a series of abstracted figures, a terrain of figural space. It is the space of a floating presence of light value and color which cannot be stopped at a system of connotation.

To look closely at this space, to unfold it, to stop its movement, its flows, and to examine it is to open up the story of the metaphor. In *Lemon* we find the traces make gestures towards figures, as the unified lemon is fragmented by the changing light and the passage of individual frame fragments; these figures create certain "obvious metaphors." There is the breast which appears on the right side of the lemon and becomes transformed into a phallus as the light hits only the bottom right edge. Female/male transformations played a prominent role in early cinema, as in the fascination of Méliès' *Le Prestidigateur* and were particularly evident in surrealism; certainly Freud and Lacan have suggested why this particular polarity should be the recurrent object of transformation: for sexual difference, denied or understood, it is at the basis of our experience of difference per se.[42]

We can also fantasize the story of a moon going through phases, a metaphor for temporal passing, for a cycle, an eternal return with no beginning or end. We can also see an image of transformation of day into night, which is involved in the same transformation of opposites as is the male/female metaphor. We can see in the comparison of the two a play with our frame of reference. The film then becomes a game in which the cosmological can be transformed into the partial sex object, the moon and the breast metaphorically linked in a new way—simply because they exist in the same image which has no scale references once we understand it as figural space.

In discussing the story of metaphors I was forced to move beyond metaphor into a process of transformation, perhaps better termed "metamorphosis."[43] To understand the process, it is perhaps useful to point to a film fragment by Barry Gerson called *Metamorphosis*, the last part of *Endurance/Remembrance/Metamorphosis*. Here the camera changes focus, shooting through a terrarium out a window at a wooded hill. Pulling focus transforms our space, but also our ability to fix ourselves in space as spectators. Metamorphosis, a "plastic possible" for the camera, for the film image indicates that beyond or besides representation, film can function as a process on us, can be an affect of our libidinal economy.

This brings us to a critical metaphor which tells a story about *Lemon*—the metaphor developed by Lyotard in his article, "l'Acinéma."[44] He speaks of the subject's position in classic film as the same as the client in porno photography parlors, where men have to pay to have women pose nude for their cameras. Striking a pose to be fixed in a fetishized frame, the classic film moves, but the rigidity of the limits of this movement allows this critical comparison to hold— for like the woman immobilely positioned at the photo gallery or the woman bound and chained in de Sade, the movement of the classic fiction film is marked by a restricted performance. Lyotard sees avant-garde film as breaking through the distinction in two ways. Some avant-garde films break this limitation by excess and aggression (the camera moves in all directions, shakes, the image cuts frame by frame, the effect being described by another of Lyotard's critical metaphors, pyrotechnics). Other films, like *Lemon*, break the limitation by a marked lack, a motion less than the restricted motion of the classic norm. The voyeur-customer is made as uneasy as if he were paying to photograph a corpse. *Lemon* is apparently of the second type *if* we consider the framing of the object and the camera's fixed position; but if we consider the movement of light and the changes described earlier, we see that even within the minimal, the lack, excess can be paradoxically inscribed. As lack is metamorphosisized into excess, and then the process is reversed, the figure of reversibility is introduced.

The reversed metamorphosis, excess into lack, can be seen to operate in a film like Frampton's *Autumnal Equinox*. At first this series of panning shots in closeup of the exposed animal flesh, blood, and swinging tools of a slaughter house, punctuated by green leader, seems to fit the category of excess, due to the overwhelming force of movement, color, and light intensity. The film's length and its nearly repetitive imagery, however, create out of this excess a lack of development. The shock resides, rhythms establish themselves, and we become involved in a loose pattern, a familiarity, which allows us to look intensely at what earlier seemed to be flashes evading, attacking, such a steady gaze.

Thus Lyotard's remarks on excess and lack in the avant-garde, while fruitful in introducing us to its project, need to be expanded in order to provide a closer attention to the functioning of these films. The polarity (excess/lack) needs to be rethought in relation to various aspects of filmic expression within each film and in terms of the dynamics of process, of flux, of metamorphosis (dynamics which are elsewhere fully developed by Lyotard).

Still to be considered in *Lemon* is the story of representation, especially as reinscribed by the fade to black and the blue, back light, gradually increasing, then changing to yellow. The light ceases to function as a modeling device after the fade out, as a device which allows the filmic image to represent three dimensional space. Space is flattened to equal the planar surface of the screen, the space of posters, of modern art's attention to the canvas as the surface of representation.

Imagine being able to place, side by side, the "*trompe l'oeil*" moment of *Lemon* described earlier, when the light modeled the lemon into its fullness as object, and this moment of flattening of the silhouette against a colored background. The tendency is to see the conventions of the seventeenth-century's notion of representation deconstructed, abstracted, so that the backlit silhouette is comparable to the flat areas of color defining the space of a Barnett Newman canvas. But this points to the different status of light and shadow in representation in film and in painting; the system of highlighting in painting is always just an illusion, while even the filmic approximation of flattening of space into areas of color depends, precisely, on a back light, a light source emanating from the depth of the image.

As we become aware of this light coming from behind, we realize that the image exists in the impossible meeting of this back light with the light coming from the projector lamp, the light which allows the image to exist. The "impossibility" of the meeting of these two lights is of a temporal order. It is the same temporal gulf which separates the artist and the spectator.

It is useful for the spectator to attempt to bridge this gap, to respond to the film as the emanation of a creative artist who can be reached through the film? Much of the writing on the avant-garde film depends on just this concern with the artist as a creative personality, so that the film becomes a key to the artist's "nature," his or her "development," or "influences." The maker of *Lemon* apparently invites us to undertake such a search, the exploration of a secret narrative that initiated the film and would perhaps explain his intentions. He does this by ending the images with the appearance of writing, (the only language in the film, for in the original print, the title "Lemon" never appears) an enigmatic dedication of the film, "for Robert Huot." Then again, this apparent invitation to solve a puzzle of intentionality may be "intended" as yet another joke. The point seems to be that the artist's secret narrative has now been joined by those of each of the film's viewers.

Lemon can thus be seen as an excellent example of what the avant-garde project is concerned with exploring. Changes in the process of inscription of the image attack, make reference to, and comment on the codes of pictorial representation. Within this process is the exploration of film's potential for generating energy and acting as a dynamic mechanism in an interaction with the imagination and body of the viewer.

3

Sound: Beyond Distinctions Between Music, Noise and Speech, A New Process, A New Ordering

Thus far in this inquiry into avant-garde film, I have concentrated on the image track, virtually ignoring the soundtrack. The reason in this delay in attention to sound is partially determined by the silence of many of the films I am considering. It is a silence which differs from that of the "silent films" made prior to the development of a practical mechanism for incorporating a soundtrack within the body of the film, for those films made prior to the "coming of sound" were for the most part projected with musical accompaniment. The current choice of silence in some of these avant-garde films represents a negative reaction to that historical tradition of music as a complementary and reinforcing signifying system within the filmic system, a tradition whose rules and assumptions I will explore in detail in this chapter.

The lack of added sound is embraced by these recent films as an important principle of their functioning. Silence is used "positively," not construed as a lack, but rather as a militant insistence on vision. This chapter on sound will be divided into a discussion of silence, followed by an examination of sound in avant-garde film.

Stan Brakhage appears to have had a historically significant role in positing this use of silence,[1] when after working with experimental music and sound (his own, Jim Tenney's in *Interim,* [1953] and John Cage's in *In Between,* [1955]) he turned to silence for most of his work after 1955. As a result, silence has been to a certain extent associated with Brakhage's type of filmic imagery, and more especially with the metaphoric sense of vision which permeates his own writing, (as well as critical writing on his films) and at times receives direct figuration in the films. This silence becomes associated with an inner, subjective world, an exploration of the connection between sight, memory, imagination and the unconscious.

Brakhage's intentions should not be taken as determining the function of his works. The critical attention he has received tends to closely follow his own writings, embracing the romantic poet personna that Brakhage develops behind his film work. Such an approach tends to unify and explain his imagery in terms of a system of signification far more traditional and conventional than his films actually are. His films become much more exciting when seen outside this frame.

We can see Brakhage as an experimenter with silence, who displays an understanding of the power of silence even in the rare films in which he uses sound. Such is the case with *Fire of Waters,* a film composed of what appears to be shots of lightning over night images of a suburban landscape, but is in fact discernible as a "fake" lightning effect, the result of various over and underexposed images of these houses, all shot during the day. The eerie atmosphere, increased by the tension of a representation whose "veracity" is in question, is augmented by a soundtrack nearly devoid of sounds except for: (1) wind rising in pitch at the very beginning; (2) slowed-down bird sounds in the middle and (3) the speeded-up sound of a woman giving birth, rerecorded at two levels. My source of identification of these sounds is Brakhage himself, for one can not identify, upon an initial hearing, what sounds are used as sources.[2] This abstraction raises the question of how one can then speak of any referential or representational function. Here Brakhage's use of sound concentrates on sparcity and abstractness. He uses sound to accentuate the tension of his formal manipulation of the image. The resultant disturbance of representation occurs differently and simultaneously within two expressive matters, a parallel tension which escapes the redundancy of accompaniment.

Analysis of Brakhage's other films would similarly show that it is possible to construe his use of silence as not only signifying interiority of vision, but also as functioning to emphasize the exploration of the physical properties of cinematographic registration. A corollary of the exploration of registration is, as I developed in the last chapter, an opening up of representation and an exploration of the inscription of force.

It is this later project that is common to other filmmakers who use silence. They avoid a competition of sound with the image and any attempt to "add" to the image by including sound. The resonance they gain for the image projected in silence is joined by the option of shooting and projecting their films at 16 frames per second. A slower rate of change of individual film frames through camera and projector mechanisms allows for a greater perception of light and motion variation. For films like those of Barry Gerson, Larry Gottheim and Hollis Frampton, where sensitivity to light and motion is centrally important, this slower, silent speed in certain works becomes a tool in the exploration of kinetics and luminosity.

The absence of a soundtrack does not necessarily indicate absolute silence; if the films are projected (as 16mm prints often are) without a soundproof booth, the silence is colored by the presence of the sound of the projector mechanism. Erasing, overshadowing this noise was one purpose of the musical accompaniment of the early silent films, as has been widely noted by film historians:

> It [film music] began, not as a result of any artistic urge, but from the dire need of something which would drown the noise made by the projector. For in those times there were as yet no sound-absorbent walls between projection machine and auditorium. This painful noise disturbed the visual enjoyment no small extent. Instinctively cinema proprietors had recourse to music, and it was the right way, using an agreeable sound to neutralize one less agreeable.[3]

We saw in the last chapter how the camera mechanism was developed to mask its technological production of the codes of perspectival vision; now we can add to this masking operation a sound mask meant to cover the functioning of the projection apparatus. The avant-garde films are not afraid of their audience hearing the projector noise. As studies of how the film apparatus can manipulate light and motion, they have no great investment in making us any less aware of any part of that apparatus.

In accord with this last point is the notion of a "musical" aesthetic of silence, as prominently championed by contemporary composers such as John Cage. Cage sees one progressive role for the musician as performing silences during which the audience is invited to listen and to itself perform. Nam June Paik in his videotape work, *Tribute to John Cage*, captured Cage's performances in the streets of New York in which the principles of silence, chance, noise and audience activity combine to create the separate movements of this musical work. These principles are expressed in Cage's statements in *Silence:*[4]

> There is no such thing as silence. Something is always happening which makes a sound. (p. 191)

> We need not fear these silences. We may love them. (p. 110)

> Whether or not I make them there are always sounds to be heard and all of them are excellent. (p. 152)

Silent avant-garde films open auditory space to attention, and this audial space changes with each projection situation.

I will return to these silent films for a detailed analysis of their functioning. As we move on to a discussion of the avant-garde use of sound, it is important to keep in mind that the choice of silence can be a radical theoretical gesture.

In the first chapter we considered how the avant-garde project could be usefully defined in reference to the tradition and standards of the classic narrative film and the modernist departure. A similar tracing of the history of filmic soundtracks will be equally useful in our definition and analysis of the avant-garde use of sound.

The sound which accompanied the silent film was for the most part music, at first limited to piano and sometimes harmonium, later becoming various sized orchestras depending on the size and location of the theatre operation. Kurt London, in his 1936 book, *Film Music* divided the musical production of the silent period into two categories: the compiled music used to illustrate scenes (often well-known tunes, pieces previously written) and original compositions, usually reserved for large budget films.[5] The compiled music was in fact catalogued (several handbooks and anthologies were published) and categorized according to its programmatic expression, yielding such fascinating labels as "uncanny agitato," "disturbed masses, tumult," and "bachantic." In many cases the original compositions remained involved in a similar project of programmatic music, seeking to connect the impressionistic or expressionistic significations of given musical passages to the narrative line of film, sometimes including sound effects within the orchestration as in the sound track of Murnau's *Sunrise*. It is important to emphasize that while musical scores written for films outside the Hollywood tradition often made use of compositional principles which were at the fore of the then contemporaneous musical practice, (Satie's music for *Entr'acte*, Meisel's scores for *Potemkin* and *Berlin, Portrait of a City*), most silent film music inscribed a practice of highly coded and standardized formulas. These codes can be considered as analogous to the editing pattern developed for scenic representation that marked Hollywood film style; while the editing codes insure an imaginary placement for the viewer in a scene clearly defined spatially and temporally, the musical codes create an emotional dramatic (or comic, satiric) involvement that is, in effect, equally a placement, an alignment, a marking of the boundaries of confinement.

This role assigned to music extends the sound film in the form of nondiegetic or "background" music; actually this audio regulation becomes a more complex operation due to the increasing time, money and artistic effort alloted composition and synchronization of music for sound film.

This music is usually isomorphic with the narrative developments, and the system of classic film music is often no more subtle than the stereotyped musical symbolism that fills sad scenes with plaintive violins. However the systems can get more complex than mere emphatic redundancy. Contrasting music can be used, but such irony rarely occurs in nondiegetic music. Instead, it is usually anchored in the scene by such mechanisms as the record or jukebox continuing to play frivolous music as someone is killed (a memorable example is the player piano in the scene in which the informer is murdered in Duvivier's *Pépé Le Moko*).

Beyond merely corresponding thematically to the movement of the diegesis, nondiegetic music functions importantly for pacing and rhythm, punctuation and liaison in ways that are more abstract than merely "supporting" the diegetic mood or action. Many classic scores also employ complex systems of musical motives, theme music with reprises and variations, which become a significant factor in the creation of unity. For these reasons, the nondiegetic music can be seen as playing an important structural role, which instead of being conceptualized as "background" can be considered a skeletal apparatus. This skeletal form is an abstract pattern of introductions, developments, repetitions and returns of musical moods and rhythms which the diegesis fleshes out into more concrete narrative particulars. This internal musical structure is rarely analyzed, except in cases where scores call attention to themselves through their flamboyance, as in film musicals or Bernard Hermann's scores for Hitchcock.

Turning to the other elements of the sound track, it becomes evident that they are even more intensely determined by the diegetic articulations of the film. In the classic cinema there are virtually no instances of the use of nondiegetic noise, as is even inscribed in the name Hollywood assigns to noise, "sound effects," that is, effects of narrative actions. These noises play a fundamental role in extending the scenographic space "off screen" both in ambient noise and through significant occurrences off screen which find representation on the sound track alone, either temporarily or entirely. The same holds for dialogue, although there is the possibility of voice-over narration, which as the emphatic narrating voice, then appears to control, to call into being, the images and other representations that comprise the narration in films without such voice-over modes.

The parameters which I have described as defining the dialogues, noise and diegetic music components of classic film sound tracks do not prohibit imaginative, creative possibilities of sound inscription. On the contrary, through selection, accentuation and repetition, as well as patterns or variations of pitch, tone, rhythm, intensity and volume, these auditory elements remain open to complex orchestration.

The modernist sound track establishes itself (as we saw was the case with the image) as a site of rupture with these principles of control and combination. The introduction of electronic music and the electronic production and manipulation of sounds are often used in modernist films as a blurring of the distinction between nondiegetic music and sound effects. Both of these are often used as punctuation and accentualtion of the already discontinuous style of narrative and visual description, as Michel Marie points out in discussing Resnais's *Muriel:*

> The restructuration of codes in *Muriel* is characterized by the significant status it accords manufactured sound effects prolonged by musical interventions. The recorded film music, definitively placed, is used as a material that the other effects render dynamic. This music is thus as much constituted by the instrumental music as such as by the network of relations

that operate between this music and the totality of the so-called "realistic" interventions (boat sirens, car motors, footsteps, etc.). The relation between these different materials is always dynamic, operating by progressive passages and diverse translations from one level to another, notably by the musical reprise in the bass line of the prolonged sound of the boat siren and vice-versa.[6]

This type of blending is characteristic of Fano's sound tracks for Robbe-Grillet and Rivette. The arbitrariness and tension possible in sound mixing, the extreme possibilities for selection of certain sounds and the deletion of others, cacophony and extreme inaudibility, becomes the principles of the modernist sound tracks of Godard's films, especially *Two or Three Things I Know About Her*. Some modernist films (Rochas', for example), have even been constructed as musical texts, with the whole film structured by nondiegetic musical development.

The sound manipulation within these films remains within the borders of its narrative, and while many of the sounds are new, their function in the film is still fairly conventional. As Marie puts it in his analysis, each form of musical intervention "has a very precise function."[7] For example, Marie analyzes the lyrical, sung passages whose words are unrecognizable as accentuating the abstract qualities of the human musical voice; they link the montage sequences of Hélène in nonverbal situations of solitary travel or preoccupation. Similarly, Marie points out that the instrumental nondiegetic music has a double thematic correspondence, linking on one hand "Hélène's past, the war of '39-45 and the destruction of Boulogne," and on the other hand "the character of Muriel, tied to Bernard's Algerian experience."[8] It is no wonder that Marie concludes his remarks on the relation of the filmic system and the musical system by citing Mitry's proscriptive theory of film music:

> It's not that music would be without use, but that its role is altogether different. It should not comment upon the image, nor paraphrase the expression by sustaining its rhythm— except in exceptional cases. *And even more, it should not be valued or signify for itself*. Good film music can be devoid of a musically worthy structure, provided that *in the film*, its intrusion at a given moment, has a precise signifcation. Film music is not explication or accompaniment; it is an *element of signification* and nothing more, but it draws all its force in relation to other elements: images, sounds, words.[9]

One of the problems with this theoretical formulation is that it assumes subservience of the soundtrack to the image, or at least a unified system of signification.

An exception to this assumption can be found in the contemporary narrative expression of certain European filmmakers who, through their reworking of image/sound relationships, can be considered as producing a kind of avant-garde expression. The filmic practice of such filmmakers as Straub/Huillet and Marguerite Duras differs from that of *Muriel*, for example, in that the sound track bears a much stronger role in creating narrative out of images which appear to lack a narrative development. In Duras's pair of films, *India Song* and *Son Nom de Venise en Calcutta Désert,* which share the same sound track, but have extremely different image tracks, the sound track has a highly autonomous status, which then affects our viewing of the two sets of images. To truly speak of "autonomy" though, we must discard the question of hierarchies of significantion and think of the plurality and the relationships of signification and think of the plurality and the relationships of signification as far more complex than is implied by recourse to the term "system" or even "systems."

This bring us to a defintion of the avant-garde soundtrack. Not only does it radically depart from the use of sound to fulfill a narrative progression of images and actions and from the structural uses as reinforcement of thematic developments, but the avant-garde sound track its audial characteristics as themselves worthy of attention, as the site of creative activity and expression. Through such principles as extreme disjunction, autonomy, an attack on sonic iconography, an attack on programmatic, dramatic musical structures, a play with the blending of categories of words, noise and music, the avant-garde sound track defies analysis as an element of signification *within* a system, and forces us to consider the radical plurality of the text. In other words, the breakdown and/or away from the hierarchical role of narrative as determinant "source" of sound and image gives sound a new relationship to image, to the production of signification and finally to the generation of a "narrative" as I spoke of it in relationship to *Lemon.* It's as if our theory has to turn Mitry's inside out; the sound track, to be considered avant-garde, should be valued and should signify for itself. Its precise signification is perhaps indeterminate, but its force and its range of significations should multiply the expressive force and signification of the film.

I said above that one principle of avant-garde sound track could be autonomy and disjunction, but on the contrary, there are some avant-garde films that display a high degree of correspondence between sound and image. It is likely that in these cases the sound track determines the image track, but in a manner at once more abstract and more direct that "narration," the most striking example of which are the generation by oscilloscopes or computer/video systems of images that result from the input of electronic sound, or sound notation.

Developments in technology have made certain changes available; in a sense each new lens, film stock, microphone, or tape mixing system changes the base conditions of the filmic process. Yet this is not meant to imply that each new element of technology produces "superior" or even theoretically "new" principles. It is often the case that earlier, more manual techniques closely approximated technologically mechanized ones. For example, Mary Ellen

Bute's single frame hand drawn geometric abstract films of the fifties are quite similar to the Whitneys' computer generated/cathode ray tube projected abstracts of the sixties and seventies. Still, there is a process by which changes in the technological apparatus are coupled with theoretical and ideological changes in the principles of image and sound generation and recording. This process is continually providing new terrain for avant-garde experimentation. This is particularly true as concerns the sound track, as the avant-garde embraces the nonmimetic, abstract qualities of electronic and computer-generated sound, and the time dissection, collages, and repetitions possible through changing tape speeds, directions, multi-tracking and looping.

So in order to understand the avant-garde sound track we must first see it as a change from the classical and modernist sound track tradition in which sound is a nonautonomous element within a signifying system bound to a dominant narrative mode, but we must also ask, now is this film sound, experimental sound? That is, how is it experimental in its theory of acoustics and order? How is it experimental in its exploration of the creative possibilities of new sound technology? Following from these questions we can ask, how does the theory of contemporary music, new principles of sound's relationship to language and language's grounding in articulated, yet still gestural, sound, speak to sound's autonomous activity in the avant-garde film?

No longer is it a matter of three distinct sound tracks or sound materials: noise, music and dialogue; the theoretics of the avant-garde sound track push towards "sound events" potentially forming a sound composition.

With the image track it is useful to investigate contemporary theories of painting and the photographic image and their relationship to literary theories of the production of meaning and the circulation of force. For the investigation of sound a parallel move will lead us to examine how contemporary theories of music have explored music as a semiotic system, and also as an apparatus affecting the subject's libidinal investment.

A major transformation of music theory is taking place in the consideration of music as composed of acoustic signs. Music history is no longer an independently developing realm in which greater composers create masterpieces and make purely formal innovations, but rather the history of an expressive form whose changes exist in a complex relationship to changing social and ideological structures (at once engendering, indicative and resultant). It becomes possible to trace the shifts from one representational system to another, and seek explanations for those changes.

Given this historical approach, the direct concern for an investigation of avant-garde film is the examination of the change occurring in the twentieth century. The harmonic, polyphonic system of expression of European music is replaced by a new conception of music that critiques the tradition as it evolves its own process of expression.

To speak of the theory of contemporary experimental music is to speak of a theoretical split between serial composition and process-music. The tenants of each and the resultant theoretical tension between them are not only relevant to the discussion of the sound track, but to avant-garde film in general.

Serial music proposes a new order, new principles of composition, and thus demands, at least as a first approach, to be analyzed as a historical gesture. Henri Pousseur views the serial method as having provided a systematic means of redistribution in which the mathematical basis of the musical operation gives the composer a new mechanism of production. And although the composer still applies rules to compose, the results of these operations were genuinely experimental in that they could not be anticipated in the composition process. The serial method accents extremes of sound production and combination.

Although Pousseur will defend the apparent anarchy of serial music as "cleansing action,"[10] he is concerned with a tendency towards "nondifferentiation," a nonexpressive sameness in serial composition:

> Even though the sound materials of Boulez's *Structures* are well defined in their various aspects (pitch, attack, etc.), the continual use of all possibilities, including the most contrasting juxtapositions (of registers, for example) creates a rapidly exhausting capacity of renewal, a rudimentary variation of potential, a truly structural silence, at least in respect to these characteristics. The same remarks migh be applied in a different way to the electronic piece mentioned above: if we mix enough of these timbre-dots together, we quickly arrive at a state of advanced entropy, in which all the possible structures are practically the same. The final result is one of those colored surfaces which present nothing more than the vaguest degree of articulation: either the details distribute themselves according to a sort of approximate, statistical repetitive pattern or there are imperceptible modulations, ill-defined and continual.[11]

The problem that Pousseur points to here concerns what the "very dense and rapid articulations" of this music can mean to the auditor who is not able to reconstruct any system of meaning in the work, and who may not even be able to hear (both physically and cognitively) the variations. With additional support of physiological data on audial perception, Leonard Meyer, in his book, *Music, the Arts and Ideas,*[12] makes a similar strong argument against total serialization of music. Meyer entertains the idea that such perception is to a certain extent "learned" and culturally determined, but argues that those musical events which "conform to the Gestalt laws of pattern perception (the principles of good continuation, closure, return and the like)—laws which are themselves perhaps reflections of the neuro-psychological organization of the central nervous system" have the advantage of conforming to what he calls "the natural modes of cognitive order." Gestalt psychology, as I discussed in the last chapter in relationship to perception of the visual image, is the basis of a proscriptive aesthetic position. In that discussion I indicated that conversely one can suggest that the significance of artistic expressions which do not conform to gestalt patternings is to evoke an undifferentiated perception, which in this case would mean also the perception of other qualities.

Nicholas Ruwet launches as attack on the serialist composers which is similar to Meyer's, although his point of departure is a discussion of the relationship of music to language where he applies the rules of structural linguistics as a frame. His complaint is that he finds the majority of serial compositions to be "a failure at language, at discourse."[13]

Whereas the generalization of serial principles of composition by post-Weberian composers to various characterics of sound beyond tonality (frequency, duration, amplitude, timbre) could be considered the development of an increasingly complex exploration, Ruwet maintains that the result is parallelism and conformity in these domains. Ruwet regrets the loss of "different subsystems" in which "much more complex relationships, relations of mutual implication, complementarity, compensation, etc."[14] would be found. The lack of these subsystems is regretted as a lack of a necessary articulated order, and the music is charged with appearing anarchistic and confused.

Pousseur's answer is to suggest that much of this music, especially more recent compositions, do have regulatory elements. These can be reprises of certain traditional formal and figural traits such as rhythm, harmony and symmetry.[15] Elsewhere he will suggest that regulatory elements may be born of the specific properties of electro-acoustics and computer/synthesizer sound generation.[16] Thus the auditor will need to be made aware of the "active creative aspects of elementary acoustics" and will learn to recognize that in this new music there is an exciting lack of demarcation between the international composition of a sound and higher levels of composition. All sound events are the result of the process of determination of a multitude of acoustic qualities and each quality or aspect of sound can be submitted to rigorous composition.

It is perhaps not fully satisfactory to answer these charges that a lack of a signifying order of discrete oppositions reduces the value of this music by merely indicating the recognizable signifying orders which can be introduced.

By returning to Ruwet, we can now see that his position on serial music is marked by his attitude towards the "confused undifferentiated and ineffable" expression which exists "beneath or beyond language: cries, glances, caresses, etc.,"[17] in other words, precisely what constitues the "gestural" in Kristeva's theory. Music for Ruwet must not approach the "anarchy" or "chaos" of these gestural systems, and it is on this basis which he attacks Pousseur's espousal of the "infinite richness of noise as compared to the relative poverty of musical sounds selected by traditional music."[18] Here Ruwet exposes the limitations of his own theoretical position and we can once again see how the rigid application of structural linguistics falters before avant-garde expressivity within a trans-linguistic system.

If some of the early serial compositions are lacking, perhaps it is because they lacked a theory of the richness of noise and of gestural expression necessary to make an exploration of the preverbal qualities of music effective. The later composers of the serial tendency have better understood that more is needed than a different system defined by rules which negate the earlier traditional order, and they are better able to seek a positive development of a new expressivity. But it is certainly with process-music that the gestural aspects of music gain theoretical attention, providing new music with a different creative design than the music of the Western tradition.

The theories of process-music were put forth in the writings of John Cage, who, as early as 1959, defined musical experimental action as limited to that which, as a result of history, becomes a necessary new move:

> One does not then just any experiment, but does what must be done; one does not seek by his actions to arrive at money but does what must be done; one does not seek by his actions to arrive at fame (success) but one does what must be done; one does not seek by his actions to arrive at the establishment of a school (truth) but one does what must be done. One does something else. What else?[19]

Cage argues that the historically new direction for the avant-garde to take is to let "sound come into its own" which for him means:

> . . . noises are as useful to new music as so-called musical tones, for the simple reason that they are sounds. This decision alters the view of history, so that one is no longer concerned with tonality or atonality, Schoenberg or Stravinsky (the twelve tones or the twelve expressed as seven plus five), nor with consonance and dissonance, but rather with Edgar Varese who fathered forth noise into twentieth century music. But it is clear that ways must be discovered that allow noises and tones to be just noises and tones, not exponents subservient to Varese's imagination.[20]

This critique of serial composition is not based on its nonarticulated expression, but instead claims that serial music retains too much of the European tradition, too much continuity with the past. Process-music counters serial music's analytic methodology by introducing chance operations and nonrepresentational graphic notation that allow for indeterminacies. Each performance is free to make impulsive choices. The process musicians (Cage, David Tudor, Christian Wolff, Morton Feldman, among others) do not necessarily strive for the production of musical discourse or the exposition of an idea of order, but play with the gestural and the process I spoke of earlier as *signifiance*.

The ideological analysis of the break constituted by contemporary music is difficult. Adorno has suggested that the break be conceived as a negative moment of a dialectic in which the dominant order is destroyed.[21] Lyotard points out in his essay, "Adorno com diavolo,"[22] that this neglects a "positive" project operative within contemporary musical practice, and that Adorno's position is marred both by a nostalgia for totalizing, lyric forms and an inability to consider a libidinal economy.

Iwanka Stoianova has attempted to elaborate such a theory of the positive aspects of new music. In speaking of the emphasis on process and gesture in this music, she draws a comparison to a similar process-oriented practice in modern literature.

Highly critical of semioticians of music who assume a linguistic model, Stoianova blasts them for paying attention only to what is "not musical in music," and therefore easy to assimilate as linguistic categories.[23] It seems that Stoianova is pointing out, as does Serres concerning painting, that even within the most traditional compositions one must still speak of processes of expression that are not linguistic, but preverbal, and therefore not subsumed under a verbal construct of signification. She directly draws on the theories of Kristeva and Lyotard I spoke of in the last chapter, urging that musical theory concern itself with how musical gestures transpose energy.

Stoianova tends to see both tendencies of contemporary music as eliminating a recourse to the traditional patterns of development and resolution, and thus placing the listener in an audial present. Reprises or traditional constructs common to some post-serial music (as I discussed earlier), are seen as a work of intertextuality, and thus part of the play with *significance.* Stoianova's analogies to Kristeva's theories on modern poetic language lead her to difficulties at this point, however, since she fails to consider that much contemporary music is constructed in a highly organized manner.

It seems that the two opposing tendencies of process and serial music can best be dealt with be a methodology which examines what is gestural and what constitutes the tradition of order in each musical work. In examining Berio's musical transposition of a poem in his article, "A Few Words to Sing, Sequenza II,"[24] Lyotard has taken on a problematic parallel to one Stoianova treats when she discusses work with Mallarmé, that is, the relationship between contemporary writing practices as an attack on the communication model of language and postserial music. Lyotard concludes that the deconstruction of language accomplished by the phonemic distortion of the poem is actually operating in opposition to the more organized articulation of the music. This constitutes a reversal of the role of language and music. Language, usually associated with secondary elaboration, is here submitted to the fragmented expressivity of the primary processes, while music, often seen as more immediately expressive, is here ordered and controlled.

Lyotard's essay is an important model of theoretical analysis, as it treats the problem of disjunctive uses of expressive matter to create both force and meaning in the interplay of these tensions and cultural expectations. Rather than fixing an ideological position for new music as a unity, the essay suggests that the range of activity, from the most impulsive, anarchistic expression of primary drives to the most regulated, mathematically precise formulations, must be analyzed as they are variously selected or placed in tension with one another.

The ideological field of possibilities opened by these extremes is immense, ranging from concrete sounds deriving from "natural" sources to synthesized sounds whose instrument of production is electronic rather than mechanical, from the computer generated "mantra" to sound blasts which approach regions of pain to human ears and evoke parallels to sado-masochistic theater.

The avant-garde sound track can thus be seen as borrowing from the principles of contemporary music in defining its practice of sound composition, as well as reacting against the signifying order of the traditional sound track. The following six points summarize the major principles of avant-garde sound track composition derived from this dual impetus:

1. A blending of the categories of noise, music and words. This can simply take the form of treating "noises" (so defined by the irregularity of vibrations) as material worthy of musical attention. It can also mean using words as the material of composition in a form radically different from the "lyric." An example is Steve Reich's compositions, "It's gonna rain," and "Come out to show them," in which tape-recorded phrases (an evangelist preacher in the first instance and a young black man arrested in a riot in the second) are submitted to "phasing." This involves the same phrase on loops on different recorders being thrown out of synchronization, so that the delay causes overlaps, echoes, etc. Portions of the phrase are staggered and several phases are overdubbed, multiplying the basic phasing effect. In Reich's tapes the phrase is in unison at the beginning and end, creating an intriguing contrast between these moments and the high degree of distortion and abstraction in the middle, a distortion which is the result of the phasing accenting "acoustic incidentals":

> ...acoustic incidentals in the original loops—such as the sound of pigeons heard in the background behind the preacher's voice, verbal transients, consonants and so on—are released, emphasized and transformed by the repetition and phase-shifting process, adding a dimension of previously unheard and unsuspected sounds which could not have been produced in any other way.[25]

Thus words are abstracted from their signifying function, as attention is shifted both to the gestural patterns of their utterance and the mechanism of a new musical process.

2. The tension between order and anarchy, between serial foundations and process theoretics of chance and expressivity. This was developed in the above discussion of Ruwet, Pousseur, and Cage. Avant-garde sound tracks can be of

either extreme, or they can contain both extremes, as Lyotard's analysis in
dicated operating in the Berio piece. To call it a "tension between extremes"
may be misleading, for it does not indicate the difference from the tension
operative in all music, even the most classic, but especially the romantic and
expressionist mode. This problematic within avant-garde practice must be seen
as existing between a "new order" and a rebellion against all order, as discussed
earlier.

3. Experiments with electro-acoustics. First there is the possibility of
generation of various types of sound waves, including the sinusoidal wave,
whose fundamental form produces no accompanying harmonics, and
therefore sounds different than musical notes. Each of the various nonsine
waves, named after their oscillograph patterns (sawtooth, rectangular, square,
triangle) has distinct harmonic properties. These can then be filtered,
modulated, mixed or overdubbed. There are also subtractive operations of
sound generation in which white noise, containing all frequencies, is filtered in
various ways. Consider just one possibility of electro-acoustic experimentation, what Stockhausen called "internal composition"[26] that is, the ability to
compose all the internal characteristics of a given sound, and explore what he
terms the "temporal micro-structure of sonic vibration." This led him to
postulate a correlation between what we normally conceive of as rhythmic
structures and the internal oscillations of audible vibrations. Much of his
composition is directed at exploring this correlation by seeking out extremes
(with sine waves) in which internal sonic composition becomes recognizable
rhythmic structures. Another example of electro-acoustic composition is the
control of the "sound envelope," that is, the contour of sound wave amplitude
during the duration of the sound. Whereas mechanically produced musical
notes all possess a contour characteristic of the instrument of production,
synthesized sound can play with the quality of the attack, the sustaining
duration, and the decay of a sound, its envelope. Duration can be greatly
expanded, or a single sound can get progressively louder, end abruptly, etc. A
new realm of manipulation of acoustic laws, previously closed as
impossibilities, has been opened to exploration, play, composition. The avant-
garde sound track can utilize these new properties:

> Surely it is in the domain of temporal control that the electronic medium represents the most
> striking advance over performance instruments, for such control has implications not only
> for areas which are normally and primarily termed "rhythmic" but for all other notation of
> frequency succession, time rate of change or intensity, and important components of what is
> perceived in conjunction as tone-color, such as envelope...and deviations of spectrum,
> frequency and intensity during the quasi or genuinely steady state.[27]

4. Extreme repetition (minimalism)/extreme variation (asymmetry). Here I am pointing to a tendency toward structural extremes parallel to those I discussed in relationship to camera movement and editing in the avant-garde film image. We have already seen the reaction to a seemingly anarchistic music characterized by its asymmetry, its jumps in register, its lack of transitions, its inclusion of any sound. The opposing tendency of minimalism is often explained as derivative of an interest in Eastern music, but the electronic manipulations can undercut the similarities. Terry Riley's music provides an excellent example of this tendency, as is evident in this description of his "Keyboard Studies," done as a solo performance with tape loops:

> A series of fifteen short curling modal "figures," each centered around three or four notes of the mode, are each repeated a limitless number of times. . . . A solo performance may draw the figures through a very fine line of sound, where everything is "reduced" still further to an intensive exploration of the changes brought about by the repetition and combination of the pitches, as they successively rise in pitch to cover the interval of an octave—always in relation to the permanent melodic "fundamental" of the mode in bass. The multi-repetition gives each figure an independent rhythmic, melodic and accentual profile: repetition brings out these inner stresses, which are, however, purely localized, setting up tiny eddies in the onflowing continuum from which any other sort of stress or edge, is excluded. Within a completely static musical "environment" is perpetual motion.[28]

Film sound tracks, in beginning to explore either of these extremes, call upon a different sort of attention than is usually devoted to them, an attention which can listen to sound without patterned articulation on one hand, and without large scale development on the other.

5. Extreme disjunction/autonomy of the sound track, collage of disparate elements. This was discussed earlier when I considered the historical question of the avant-garde as distinguished from modernist sound tracks. Let me add that we are often dealing here with a sound track which remains highly representational, but its source, and sometimes it referent, is radically disjunct from the image track.

6. Extreme conjunction (engendering of the image track). This also was discussed earlier, as the special case in which the image is produced by sound waves being fed from an ascilloscope into a cathode ray tube, or the sound notation being part of the computer program generating the image. In both cases we are "seeing sound" instead of "hearing images," More than this simple reversal qualifies this operation as avant-garde, however, for what needs to be analyzed in each instance is how the abstact patterns generated enter into the problematic discussed as point two above, that is, the tension between order and impulses.

Experimentation with the film sound track in these avant-garde directions has only just begun, and even the fascinating work on sound in current films but suggests how much more territory is yet to be covered.

I am now going to analyze the use of sound in a few films, selected because they present widely varied examples of sound's possible function. Then in the chapters which follow, discussion of the sound tracks will be an integrated part of the analysis of the films in question.

Critical Mass (Frampton, 1970) begins with a blank screen and the whirring noise of tape on a recorder. Then a male voice begins, "OK. How are you?" The female voice responding says, "Just fine," with bitter sarcasm, not once, but identically, three times. In the dialogue which ensues between these two voices, there is a "phasing" technique similar to that described operating in Reich's phase tapes, but in *Critical Mass* the phasing occurs in a progressive series of phrases that remain an easily intelligible dialogue, except that each utterance is broken into fragments a few words long and repeated two or three times. When the image appears it is stark, high contrast black and white depicting a young woman on the right, a man on the left, both dressed in black against a plain white background. They are sharply lit from the front, casting very dark, sharply defined shadows on the wall. Their images are synchronized to the pattern of fragmentation and repetition established in the dialogue. The breaks and repetition accentuate both the verbal and physical gestures of the couple; a rise in voice is visually accompanied by an outstretched palm, a flat statement, lacking conviction, accompanied by a turning away. But the fixed frame, the harsh and spare mise-en-scène, the bright light and sharp shadow remove the couple from a temporal and spatial reality; the audience is allowed to scrutinize them as if they were suspects at a police line-up or subjects of some scientific experiment. Besides emphasizing gestural expression, the sound phasing brings to our attention the syntactic organization of their discourse; although the content is a dispute, the expression is perfectly matched. Both participants sound amazingly alike, sharing speech patterns, vague, evasive phrases that fill time, like "I mean, you know." On another level a phrase like this encapsulizes the whole discussion, the "I-you" antagonism, the discrepancy between an intended massage and a received interpretation. The parallelism of their verbal moves is again accented by the breaks, as can be seen in the following exchange (each fragmented segment is repeated twice):

Her: What am I/a piece of shit/you don't tell me
Him: I'm sorry / but I didn't / have the time
Her: Well what / were you / so busy doing
Him: It was/ a very/spontaneous thing

A structural shift occurs; the image is interrupted by white frames, then the white circles which indicate the end of a reel of film stock. Then the black and white frames alternate with the image as before. Now the sound also changes its phasing so that a phrase like "none of your business" can get staggered as "none of your / your business / isness. Another intriguing aspect of the phasing is its play on the sexuality of the exchange through an ambiguous chopping off of phrases containing such sexual epithets as "fuck" and "screw"; for example, the phrase "If you're not willing to fuck / ing trust me" gets punctuated so that the "hidden" signification, "If you're not willing to fuck" resounds.

Another structural shift begins with the voices becoming very soft. Again, the symmetry/contrast between parts played by each voice is underlined in the repetition of "you know /fuck you." In the soft tone, underscored by crying, her voice says, "I don't know how / much longer / I can keep doing it," a phrase that by this point in the film attains considerable irony as "it" could be the relationship, the argument, or the film itself. The sound track becomes just "oh/ah" sighings, but then the phrase phasing returns.

Shift again for a segment where the entire image turns grey, accompanied by the only period of silence in the film. The silence and blank image puctuate the film, the most pronounced example of a structural demarcation. This void draws our attention to the structuration of the film as a series of segments distinguished from one another by shifts in the sound/image patterns, in the phasing technique, in synchronization or asynchronization and in image qualities.

The overall concerns of the film are thus structural as well as gestural; or to be more explicit, the structure serves to create and emphasize the gestural and playful aspects of this pseudo-clinical dissection of human discourse and filmic discourse. Speech and film are both submitted to this deconstruction and recomposition, and the silence on all levels emphasizes this interrelated activity.

The voices return, very soft, their utterances indistinguishable. A line appears, bisecting the screen just left of center, first black, then white. This line remains when the image of the couple reappears. The line serves as a transition between its abstract appearance in the empty image and its function in the representational image to underscore the barrier between the arguing figures, who remain on their own sides of the line.

The sound is now a stuttering echo repeating the end of phrases. Then the sound, with lines of dialogue intact, goes out of sync, first slightly, then so much that the woman appears to be voicing the man's part. The voices come together in normal conversation. This out-of-sync interlude functions along with the tape recorder noise to make the audience at once aware of the mechanical processes of sound recording and the dominance of the sound in this film. The out-of-sync segment also performs a role transformation, suggesting that the dialogue parts are exchangable, just as the "logic" of the arguments crossover from one character to another. This sense of return, echo, repetition and interchangeability within the argument is also presented by the return of whole phrases of dialogue from the beginning of the film in these last sections.

These echoes and transformations occurring on both a "diegetic" and compositional level create an element of a joke, the same kind of double edge that occurs when the woman, who is told by the man to "get out," backs out of the frame.

"Critical mass," a title which literally means "the smallest mass of fissionable material which will sustain a nuclear reaction," points to the explosive energy released in an argument or inscribed by a filmic expression of phasing, repetition and structural contrasts (the pyrotechnics discussed in the last chapter). Or "critical mass" could mean a ritual of criticism, a vital ritual, a critique of matter (subject matter by a staggered filmic enunciation).

This last interpretation of the title suggests how the film plays with a narrative situation which is ideologically loaded; references abound to a social reality, as illustrated by the sarcastic line, "poor little woman at home," just one example of how the film's dialogue grounds itself in the tension of the woman's movement, sexual conflict, fidelity, honesty, etc. The film's structuration can be seen as constituting a critique, not just in the sense of negative commentary, but as an examination of the mechanisms of social behavior.

The techniques of process music are transfered to the graphics and kinetics of the images and the arguing figures represented in these images. Images are edited to correspond to the phasing of the sound track. But the "acoustic incidentals" which receive accentuation through Reich's phasing technique are perhaps supplanted here by a more ordered reiteration, more structured changes, less chance occurrences. The question of order in *Critical Mass* remains highly problematic, since there is no developmental logic in the film's division into sections of different patterns and each section seems to drift into the next. Finally, the film can be seen as a close approximation of process composition.

A quite different approach to sound is illustrated by Robert Breer's film, *Blazes.* Here the animation, frame by frame, of various sketches done in an abstract expressionist style, including traces of calligraphy, is accompanied by a sound which recalls water gurgling down a drain. The visual frames repeat, but apparently randomly, and are at times surrounded with black frames. Close to the end of the film, a series of zooms forward on the drawings is accompanied by a clicking noise. As the images in the first section of the film change either every frame or every two frames, they are not registered as separated images, but as superimposed, changing compositions. For example, a red diagonal stroke may appear superimposed on a yellow circular design only to be later part of a series of blue squiggles. The rapid variation of changing designs and color, the composition of highly energized abstract shapes in continual transformation and the illusionary game of presence or absence of any given image (since the "mixing" happens perceptually rather than physically on the film's footage), give the film its power as figural space in the Lyotardian sense.

The zooms towards the end of the film are disconcerting due to the abstract image plane which is their focus; they give the illusion not only of movement towards the images, an attempt to penetrate and invade that surface, but also of the imagery itself moving forward at the viewer, as it rapidly gets larger. The realm of visual energy thus far established is intensified in these quick pulsings of a new dynamic space towards the end of the film.

The sound is as nonrepresentational as the image—water is not so much a referent as a possible fantasy evoked by the strange sound. There is only one major articulation in the sound track, the change from "gurgling" to "clicking" which corresponds with the change in the image from the rapid succession of changing frames to the zooms; within each of the two parts, the sound is highly repetitive. The sound track accompanies the image track's structure, but only as parallel changes in abstract expressions.

Blazes serves as an example of how a filmic sound track can let noise be heard apart from an effect of signification or representation. The sounds in *Blazes* may have "natural" sources, but they are heard as auditory pulses devoid of specific references, opening the space of auditory fantasy. The auditor becomes sensitive to the repetition, and the structural shift. The mystery of identification of the sound has its own intrigue, but the "closer" one listens, the more conscious one becomes of the noises' qualities, their patterns, their energies. These discoveries gradually supplant the desire to "know" the sound as an icon. The force of this sound is released by its parallel to the figural space of the image. The title "Blazes" can be interpreted as suggesting a concept very similar to the trace, the linkage of an inscription in an artistic practice with the psychic apparatus' mode of registration. The film constructs a duration which is only minimally articulated as a structuration of time. Traces pass through this duration repetitiously and dynamically. The calligraphic suggestions found in the imagery are graphic traces of a writing practice, but one which is indecipherable in any direct sense. It is a collection of gestures, a direct presentation of force.

Crossroads, by Bruce Conner, is also concerned with sound abstraction, but uses a metamorphosis of noise effects into concrete music accompanying a repetitive series of images to open different questions of the relationships of force and signification within filmic composition.

The film is composed of lengthy static framings from various angles of the Bikini Atoll test of the atomic bomb (official U.S. Government footage). We see the mushroom cloud explosion formed over and over again, from sea level and from the air. The sound track begins with a sync track of the explosion, which in this special case means that the explosion in the image and the noise of its occurrence do not "match." The rumbling noises are heard with a delay in respect to the image of the explosion that one would have experienced had one been at the site where the image was taken (the same delay that occurs between lightning and thunder due to the differing speeds of light and sound).

In successive images of the explosion, the sound is progressively and increasingly manipulated. First, the sound comes immediately when we see the explosion. This is scientifically speaking, impossible, placing us as spectators in an impossible spatial and temporal representation. The scientific accuracy of the delay is thus compared to the formal rhythmic impact of the false correspondence. After the midpoint of the film, marked by the appearance of a large white X crossing the screen against a black background, the sound becomes abstracted as concrete music. It retains elements of the sound of the sync track, though others are added. The sounds are reorganized, so that the effect is abstract, increasingly removed from the referent which remains in evidence in the image.

Crossroads raises extremely disconcerting questions about the relationship between cultural significations of sound and image, iconographic interpretation, and the force of a filmic expression. It captures a repeated visual release of energy, clouds of grand, billowing, expanding dynamics, coupled with an intriguing rumbling explosion sound whose reverberating patterns are abstracted into a rich and mysterious web of sound. How to reconcile our pleasure with our horror? How to reconcile force with signification? Can the force of expression so disturb a sign system as to dislocate signifiers from cultural coding? It is the abstract composition of the sound that forces these questions on an otherwise easily read image. The force of this expression exceeds and negates predetermined meanings, establishing *Crossroads* as an investigation of the symbol. This particular question will return in chapter 5 in the discussion of some films by Hollis Frampton that function similarly.

Serial composition of a sound track is much more prevalent in video art and finds its way into film through kinoscoping, the transfer of video to film. This is because the video image is not the uniform image of film, but the composite of electronically controlled impulses which can be internally articulated in serial compositions. The same program can be simultaneously displayed as visual and auditory series. One can properly speak of inversion, retrograde and retrograde-inversion forms. The rules of serial composition can be applied to patterns in the electronic image in increasingly exact and minute articulations as the technology achieves refinement of its control of temporal and spatial alterations. The attempt to combine the film image with serially composed sound would either have to be a disjunctive relationship or a mechanical approximation of serial principles to film editing, but in this case one would be restricted to frame to frame changes.

I will conclude this chapter on the use of sound in avant-garde film by emphasizing that I have tried to avoid restricting what sound should do in these films by emphasizing the multiplicity of functions it can perform.

As Stoianova points out, music (and we can add language as well), has always been involved in the gestural, but this gestural function has been subsumed and confined by rules of organization and modes of signification. Noise, on the other hand, was heard as a product of an action, evidence of its referent. The avant-garde sound track explores and expands the potential energy inherent in combinations of sounds and their juxtaposition to images. Its project is also specific and new, an effort to cross categories and increase tensions to extremes.

4

Gradual Transformations and Subtle Changes

Isolating a phenomenon, insisting on its recognition by holding it in place for critical attention or by repetition: these are the principles by which a number of recent films fulfill the project I have proposed as defining the avant-garde. By concentrating on the very subtle transformations possible through the manipulation of camera mechanisms, light sources, and the surfaces or atmospheric spaces being filmed, these films inscribe traces of expressivity which do not signify systematically according to the traditional codes of image and sound combination in classical or modernist films. The exploration of flux, contrast and transformation in relation to precisely limited concerns (i.e., color, focus, framing, movement) is one way of emphasizing how force is inscribed in filmic perception, and how it enters into processes of signification in film.

This concentration through restriction of variables and the extended duration or repetition of an effect, while it defines a group of avant-garde films, is itself used for varying effects; as each film differs in its representational or abstract functions, the process of minimalization which heightens subtle transformations affects the spectator differently and engenders different significations in each case.

In this chapter I will examine how this process is used in the works of two well-known American filmmakers, Barry Gerson and Larry Gottheim. The theoretical question which will define the analysis of the films in question is, how does the rearrangement of the filmic apparatus necessary to produce these isolated and concentrated transformations affect filmic perception and signifying processes? This will entail an investigation of processes of cognition within visual representation and processes of visual abstraction.

In the films of Barry Gerson, the camera apparatus is modified in a number of specific ways to create this minimalist concentration on specific perceptual and illusionistic effects. Although the specificity of expression and figuration in each film gives each a distinct functioning in regard to representation and abstraction, the molding of the apparatus can be described as follows:

1. The potential analogy between the vision of the human eye and the registration of the cinematic image which the classic film has exploited to achieve its illusion of reality is evoked by these films to different ends. The type of mechanical alterations of the camera apparatus which are used in Gerson's films explore the terms of the comparison and the manner in which the two perceptual experiences recall each other.

2. Focus, light, atmosphere and framing can be played with to make recognition of objects difficult, to obscure their identity and thus emphasize abstract components of composition and texture. However, there is always a moment at which recognition is possible, at which the image is clearly representation.

3. The scene to be filmed is composed of objects, but it is fragmented and framed and reframed in ways that emphasize the division of space by strong lines and by blocks of color as in the compositions of such artists as Moholy-Nagy and Klee. Mattes can be introduced as an internal reinforcement or an addition to framing.

4. In many films the camera is fixed, but when camera movement occurs it is curved and diagonal in its motion up and down and in and out, never in a single plane as in a straight tracking shot. The camera is hand held, and movement is submitted to repetitions which create a rocking effect.

5. The films are shot and projected at speeds which vary (i.e., shot at 32 fps, slow motion and projected at 16 fps). These variations produce different perceptions of motion. They also create slight flicker effects which serve as a visual beat to be considered, along with a frequent jiggling of the image, as an element in the rhythm and duration of the films.

What effects arise from composing films according to these proscriptions? One consequence is that the film image comes to share certain sculptural principles achieved in Gerson's paracinematic sculptures. These sculptures are long boxes with binocular viewers at one end and a "scene" set up on cut-outs (some in motion) spread back through the depth of the box, with a light source or a rear projection of a film at the far end. The representation achieved involves spatial illusions and tricks, with the label "paracinematic" referring to the overlap between the sculptures and cinematic concerns. This blending of cinema and sculpture is reminiscent of Marcel Duchamp's "The Bride Stripped Bare by Her Bachelors, Even (the Large Glass)" and "To Be Looked At (from the Other

Side of the Glass) With One Eye, Close To, For Almost an Hour," assemblages, which, as Octavio Paz has pointed out,[1] turn the act of looking into a "viewing-through." It is also related to Moholy-Nagy's motorized light sculptures, what he called his light-display machines, described by Moholy-Nagy as follows:

> I dreamt of a light-apparatus, which might be controlled either by hand or by an automatic mechanism by means of which it would be possible to produce visions of light, in the air, in large rooms, on screens of unusual nature, on fog, vapor, and clouds. I made numberless projects, but found no architect who was prepared to commission a light-fresco, a light architecture, consisting of straight or arched walls, covered with a material such as galalite, trolight, chromium or nickel, which by turning a switch could be flooded with radiant light, fluctuating symphonies, while the surfaces slowly changed and dissolved into an infinite number of controlled details.[2]

Architecture, radiant light, surfaces slowly changing, an infinite number of controlled details: these same elements are at play in Gerson's films, not as a three-dimensional display as envisioned by Moholy-Nagy, but nonetheless present in these constructed film images.

The film provides for a special vision, a looking in which the potential for analogy to the eye's vision is played off against an equally strong concern with the specificity of the camera mechanisms. The representation aspects of the image, the recognizable objects and environments such as air, sea, sky, as well as curtains, windows, radiators and walls serve as a kind of lure. As reference points to our visual experience over our lifetimes, outside of film, they become a device through which the film taps an association with nonfilmic vision; yet, what is avoided is the mere reproduction and reconstruction of the visual impression the eye would receive if it were a direct witness to the locality at which the camera was placed. Through the readjustments of the camera apparatus mentioned earlier, the image is transformed into a decoy, as marked a pastiche as are the sculpture boxes.

To explain the fascination of this operation, it is necessary to refer to the Lacanian analysis of visual fascination in the trompe l'oeil discussed in chapter 2. The aim of these films is to engage the psychic processes associated with the act of vision, the drives which can be termed scopophilia. The desire to see, the pleasure to be derived from seeing are stimulated by an initial lure of representation. This representation serves as a pretext for a concentration on the abstract properties of perception, sensitivity to color, movement, definition of area and duration. The films can be analyzed as *"dispositifs"* as Lyotard has used the term to describe apparati which are designed to transform energy,[3] but can be understood more specifically as stimulating and transforming the force connected to visual drives. Displacement occurs of the kind of desire to see which functions in representational, narrative constructs (to see the nude body, to see the sex act, to see gems, treasures) onto images denying these referential systems and their ideological values.

We can see this operating in Barry Gerson's film trilogy, *Endurance/Remembrance/Metamorphosis.* The titles provide this emphasis on an abstraction quite removed from the concrete physical objects referred to in the image. All three titles refer to states of duration, but of different types, ranging from constancy, to the reemergence of the past in the present, to a process of change. The conceptual references to ways of marking or defining a period of duration are not simply illustrated by the images of the films, which is to say that nomination here is not a labeling of the correct interpretation of a metaphysical correspondence. Rather, the abstract conception of the title exists in a complex relation to the progression of images that comprise each film. A suggested meaning floats over the physical patterns of light that constitute these images of varying degrees of representationality.

In *Endurance* the image is constructed out of identifiable objects whose identity is troubled, though not obscured, by the oblique camera angle. The play of light and shadow within the reflection on the floor allows recognition of the objects within the representation. The scene can then be reconstructed as a corner of a room with a window offscreen through which light filters to cast the shadow. This spatial representation is reinforced by the bottom of the white curtains which we assume belong to the unseen window, waving in and out of the upper left corner of the frame. Interestingly, we first see the shadow, then the object, then become intrigued by the mirroring of their motion, then use these matching motions as indicators of our placement within a scene.

This withholding of delineation of the spectator's placement relative to the frame differs radically from the imaginary positioning of a spectator relative to a conventional filmic representation. Lacking a narrative context which would guarantee the legibility of this odd angle by some motivation supplied by surrounding shots (here it could be a glance/object editing pattern with a main character fixedly gazing at the floor with his/her head tilted to one side), this shot remains oblique in the metaphorical as well as literal sense.

There is a double sense in speaking of this film as the edge or border of a representational scene—literally as a corner of the room, a fragment, a spatial metonymy, but in the larger sense as a limit, a tension between representation and abstraction. Within that tension we can speak not only of visual fascination, but also of an inquiry concerning principles of perception. By examining these principles briefly, in the terms in which scientists have chosen to discuss them, the vast scope of this inquiry (which is not at all obvious due to our tendency to naturalize and take for granted the elements of visual phenomena) will become evident. By opening this area, I hope to point to another manner of seeing not only *Endurance,* but all of Gerson's film constructs.

Scientists have defined the modes of color appearance as key to our perception of objects: they are illumination (in space), surface, and film (through an aperture, the rendering of a flattened two dimensions, *not* objects in space).[4] Concerning these various modes they will speak of attributes such as hue, saturation, brightness, lightness, duration, size, shape, location, texture, glossiness, transparency, fluctuation (flicker, sparkle, glitter), insistence, pronouncedness and fluorescence. Gerson's films manipulate a sliding relationship between what would be illumination and surface modes within the representational scene and what is a film mode within the abstraction of the scene as a fragmented cinematic image.

The filmic apparatus modifies the color relationships of surface and illumination due not only to the film mode (flattening), but also due to the chemical registration properties of the film stock, and finally, the physical properties of projection of the image by a lamp on a screen. Due to the disturbance of the cognitive context discussed earlier, these perceptual differences between color appearance in film and outside film are accentuated. Play with those perceptual categories becomes part of the functioning of the film. In *Endurance,* we come to recognize the bright orange light reflected on the deep brown wood of the floor as being cast by the offscreen window, but not right away. Only when the attributes of these patches of color come close enough to the series of attributes which we recognize as referring to those objects does recognition take place. Iconic connections and the establishment of the spatial and temporal relations of the scene are delayed.

This delay in cognition has the film pose the following question: what would happen, what processes are affected and what effect is produced by manipulating the relationship of modes of color perception? What happens to the viewer in this series of transformations?

No clinically valid answer is attainable for an experiment containing so many variables; perception experiments are known for their precise control of all constants surrounding the variable of perception being measured, and when that control is impossible due to the nature of the experiment (i.e., the work of Von Senden [1960] and Gregory [1966] on the immediate organization of the visual field of cured blind people) the conclusions are questioned by many members of the scientific community.[5] Also, it is extremely difficult to devise experiments which go beyond sensory data to supply information for a cognitive theory of perception. Cognitive theories rely on extrapolation and even speculation. I am suggesting that in moving even beyond cognitive information to psychoanalytical affects and emotional response, one moves perception theory outside of the empirical bounds where it then encounters artistic theory.

Remembrance presents another example of how this matrix of perceptual operations and contextual manipulation can be presented as a filmic object of fascination for the viewer. In the case of *Remembrance,* there is a play with the mise-en-scène of filmic metaphors (a window, its frame and a reflection), as literal objects in a way that turns these metaphors inside out. The camera is positioned outside the window looking in on the room and yet this view of the interior is made difficult to discern due to the reflection of the exterior (grass, trees, sky) that covers and blends with the interior as an effect of superimposition. The collage of interior and exterior space, of transparency and mirror reflection, is not a manipulated superimposition accomplished either in the camera or in the laboratory through the printing of multiple rolls prepared for this purpose. Instead, as in Brakhage's film *The Wonder Ring,* (images taken through the windows of an elevated train of the reflections of the train in the windows of the New York City apartments it passes), the camera duplicates a possible optical effect available to the eye. The framing of the image and the camera movement in each case accentuate the disconcerting aspects of a window that operates as a mirror, since this framing and movement denies us a clear placement in space.

The theoretical metaphor that compares film to a window on the world is complicated by the introduction of a window whose figuration involves a doubling of imagery. The contact between interior space and exterior space on the window/image plane is literally all external to the viewing subject, but the strange images produced by focussing on this window/juncture recall the floating, imaginary visions that Lyotard describes in modern painting, as I discussed in chapter 2. This floating is reiterated in the image in the way the antique lamp, composed of double round glass ball shades, appears to float in space, since the reflection blocks our view of the lamp's position on a table. Also, the camera beings to move in and out in a curved motion which further emphasizes the precarious and shifting spatial relationships. Eventually, the camera movement brings the window frame into view and discloses the spatial representation that the film had previously kept enigmatic. So by enveloping the spectator in a visual apparatus of subtle changes, Gerson constitutes the screen, the visual plane, as the border between image and imaginary, where the tension of abstraction and representation, force and meaning, reside.

I have already discussed *Metamorphosis* in chapter 2 as a filmic actualization of the process beyond metaphor that I associate with the avant-garde's functiong. Together these three short films illustrate Gerson's filmic practice; they transform images gradually, through motion and changes of lighting and focus, and therefore color registration. This visual shifting is a manner of creating within a film an attention to force, as the spectator is given the duration of the film to contemplate the effects of the shifting on representation and on other signifying practices of the image.

Gerson's more recent films use mattes over parts of the image. In order to discuss the functioning of the mattes in these films, it will be helpful to discuss the historical use of the matte or "mask" in the filmic image and make some general theoretical comments concerning its function.

The matte appeared first in silent films. The iris matte, as it was called, was a circular frame of darkness which surrounded a figure, often in medium long shot, centering the viewer's attention on an actor or actress or occasionally an object, as might have been accomplished by a cut to a close-up. Iris mattes appear to have been chosen as an alternative, following the assumption that the use of close-ups potentially disoriented to the viewer, as the following anecdotal "myth" offered by Billy Bitzer in his unpublished notes, and recounted by Henderson in his book on D.W. Griffith, indicates:

> Needing some means of keeping stray light rays from entering his lens from the side and spoiling the exposure through streaking the films, a phenomenon now known as "lens flare," Bitzer rummaged through his tools and spare parts and finally came up with an old glue pot. He knocked the bottom out of the pot and fastened it over the camera lens as an improvised lens hood. It seemed to serve its purpose under the studio's artificial light when the camera lens was at full aperture. And when he tried the glue-pot device outdoors, it worked equally well. In the outdoor situation, however, the camera lens was closed or stopped down, to control the increased amounts of light. When the outdoor film was developed, Bitzer noticed that the corners of each frame were dark. The edge of the glue pot had been brought into focus, producing a rounded image instead of the usual rectangular one. Bitzer was ready to toss the film away, but Griffith recognized that accident had given them the means to throw emphasis on a single element in a scene. Further refinement of the glue-pot device led to the vignette mask, which when placed over the lens on the front of the lens hood, blacked out portions of the screen in any desired shape, usually for Griffith a circle, and left only the desired figure or object on the screen. The normal procedure was to give a full shot of the scene and then follow it with a vignette shot from the same camera position, showing only the detail that was to be highlighted. The scale of the figure in the second shot remained the same as in the first shot. Griffith employed the vignette shot increasingly during the period as an alternate method of concentrating attention to the close-up.[6]

Whether or not once accepts this colorful "first time, accidental invention" myth, the point is that the matte was conceived as an adjunct focusing device, another way of selecting and concentrating the spectator's vision. Its attraction for early cinema can also be explained by the similarity to the oval frames of cameo portraits popular at the time.

The mask eventually disappeared from classic and modernist filmic practice with the exception of the occasional self-conscious nostalgic uses (in films of Welles and Truffaut, for example), or when "justified" by the supposed rendering of a subjective view through binoculars, as in Hitchcock's *The Birds*. This perhaps indicates that as audiences became more accustomed to changes in image scale and fragmentation within representation inherent in the close-up, it was the mask which seemed obtrusive and unnecessary. However the function of the mask, blocking out part of the image, was reworked as an element of mise-en-scène. Skillful filmmakers composed images using door frames, windows, parts of buildings as masks, thereby naturalizing the device.

Mattes (both the obtrusive ones done over the image and the naturalized masking elements of the mise-en-scène) came to serve two primary functions. They indicated what was of central interest or they hid something or part of something or someone from view. As such they played with the spectator's visual drives, either by encouraging fetishism, the centering of value and desire on an object or part object, or in the other case, teased the viewer's voyeuristic tendencies by blocking that which could be seen behind the censoring barrier.

When Gerson reworks the matte as contemporary element of the avant-garde image, he calls up both visual psychic investments simultaneously, and adds to that construct a dynamic of spatial division and planar differentiation which also marks contemporary work in painting, architecture, still photography and sculpture. In this context of abstraction, however, the evocation of voyeurist and fetishist drives are detached from the ideological representations that are traditionally their focus, as I indicated earlier in this chapter. The result is a concentration on the sensuality of perception itself.

Translucent Appearances offers an instance of how this is achieved. The phenomenon being filmed through the mattes is Niagara Falls; thirty-five different shots, each from a unique angle, are presented in such a way that each image consists of a singular composition of colors and movement, presenting complex spatial constructions. The mattes used range from dark blue to light grey, remaining within the monochromatic color scheme (tints and shades of blue) which characterize the falls. They are all rectangular, forming horizontal blocks of various widths across the image.

In the first four shots, a system of reversals is constructed. Shot one has a wide grey-white band over the center of the image and a narrower dark band across the bottom; shot two places a dark band on top and a light band on bottom with the falls through the center; shot three has a dark band across the top three-quarters of the image leaving a strip of falls at the very bottom. This symmetrical reversal of the mattes gives way to shots apparently much more arbitrarily ordered. A number of shots continually displace the mattes from shot to shot in relationship to the mass of flowing water. The images close with a return to the more closely matched reversal ordering.

How much interpretive value should be assigned to these structural shifts and delineations? Without allowing ourselves any false critical assurance in the celebration of clear structural simplicities (the comfort that issues from the assumption that structure embodies the "basis" of art), we can instead indicate that within a series of changing images, reiterative changes occur which unify series of shots, separating them from other shots. The audience is moved temporally through the pattern of contrasts; this is how duration, timing, rhythm and accentuation enter the film. No longer is it as undifferentiated a film as might be assumed from a description that would constitute it as thirty-five fixed shots of relatively equal length lasting twenty-two minutes concerning the use of mattes; some of the subtlety of the affective force of the film becomes understandable in the details of its construction.

The mattes in *Translucent Appearances* "interfere" with our vision of the falls which we can locate "behind them" if we temporarily think of this film as a representational scene. Following that assumption, the mattes can be seen as functioning somewhat similarly to what I noted above as characteristic of mattes in general. That is, the presence of a matte increases the visual interest of the images by invoking curiosity concerning what exists "behind" it. At the same time attention is focussed on the more restricted and therefore more concentrated view of the falls visible through the gaps between the mattes. Due to the insistence of the placement of the mattes, we watch the details of visual patterning that mark the flow of this water, the play of the top of the waterfall against the sky, the play of water against water in the splashes at the base. The additional horizontal lines and blocks of color show us that these compositional patterns are there, already inscribed in the structure of the falls itself. As such, the film attains the conceptual power found in earthwork sculpture, where the artistic manipulation of natural forms which has been the basis of the landscape painting tradition is twisted in conception to produce a new relationship between artist and land.

As an alternative, one can resist the tendency to interpret a waterfall occupying a representational space beyond the mattes imposed in front of it. One can see the film as a diorama construction of flat foreground and moving, flowing background. Or one can simply see the blocks formed by these divisions as abstract constructions dividing up and filling space, possessing textural qualities unattainable by canvas art that performs the same abstract spatial divisions. Here, again, an attention to subtle detail emerges in the composition; the framings in one case have the curved diagonal line formed by the water come to a sharp pinpoint at the frame's edge, while in another just the wisp of a diagonal cuts across the far-right corner of the frame.

These alternatives, viewing the mattes as a construct over a waterfall, or seeing the mattes join the waterfall as a seemingly integral element of an abstract image, exist in tension throughout the film. The restructured apparatus resulting from the addition of the mattes can be seen as an intriguing parallel both in representational structure and suggestive resonance to the venetian blinds that appear in Alain Robbe-Grillet's novel *La Jalousie,* and in both his novel and film *L'Immortelle.* The slats of the blind act both to frame the vision of the outside and to block it, as well as to affect the patterns of light coming through it to the voyeur/spectator. What emerges in *Translucent Appearances* is a film engaged in the intensifying of perception and of the drives connected to the perceptual act.

In his own analysis and interpretation of his films, Gerson often speaks of seeking to create "filmic energy."[7] Glimpses and fragments of a theory of energy are present in his interviews, writings, and as I mentioned earlier, in his film titles (i.e., *Evolving, Vibrations, Movements, Floating, Dissolving*). Yet Gerson does not make the connection to psychoanalytic principles; instead he turns to mystical terminology, speaking of the mesmerizing effect of states of consciousness and spiritual energy. It is interesting to note that Freud has suggested a source for such occult, mystical beliefs as a cover for psychic formations of the unconscious.[8] It is my position that the energy Gerson speaks of can be seen as generated by the changing compositions in their evocative force within the unconscious of the spectators, and that the mystical explanation should be rejected as sealing the films within a religious ideology which would undercut their radicality as contemporary cultural phenomena. Further the reference to "spiritual energy" is external to both the representation (the objects depicted) and the functions of abstraction in the films, unless one accepts that light itself is always allegorical, always evocative of some divine or mystical inspiration. It becomes incumbent upon us to denounce the ideological heritage of the Annunciation and break with its symbolic codes. We can see light as a physical and perceptual phenomenon to be manipulated by the filmic apparatus. If the artist guards a notion of spiritual inspiration, his or her artistic expression need not be interpreted merely in relation to that ideology.

Gerson's *Luminous Zone* presents an interesting case in point. The film is composed of six sections each involved with various alterations and transformations of "still-life" objects and their composition within the frame by a process of changing light and mattes. A detailed description of each of the six sections shows how the pictorial relationships are altered throughout the duration of the projection, creating illusions, rhythmic patterns and abstractions which have the potential of stimulating a fascination open to critical analysis:

1. A dark rectangular matte frames the bright red top of a heater and the pipe connecting it to the white wall behind it. At first the light is coming from the left as the image alternates with black leader so that it rhythmically flashes on the screen. The size of the matte is changed as light and shadow change patterns across the back wall which an accompanying reduction of image scale with the matte which covers more of the projected image. The light and shadow are of a webbed pattern (like those intricate shadow effects used in film noir). The alternation of the two matte sizes gives way to a section in which the light shifts across the image in a series of fixed stages. The section closes with the rectangular frame matting out all but a small portion of

the shadow pattern on the wall, then expanding to reveal the rest of the image once again.

2. Next is an image in grey and beige tones of a radiator below a window with light hitting the top bars and curtains hanging on the far corners of the radiator. The rest of the image is dark, except for light in a rectangle on the floor in the foreground in which the radiator throws a shadow of comb-like shapes. Light is flashed on and off the radiator and a smaller scale view with the matte opening proportionately reduced is intercut in alternation. Then there is a time lapse, fast motion section which is marked by the jiggling of the curtain and the image within the frame, alternating with black frames, with the black ending the section.

3. View out a partially opened window of rooftops. There is light reflected on the window sill and sash and a difference due to refraction and filtering window. Again, there is a matte introduced, a frame which undergoes size changes with corresponding changes in scale of the image, so that a more distant view appears with the smaller frame opening. The leaves on the trees outside jiggle due to the time-lapse cinematography. The window sash changes position, operating as an internal matte. Then a series of five images ranging from a full screen view to various mattes are repeated, with black leader punctuating each new series; then the five-image series is seen in inverted order.

4. The corner of a building seen against a bright blue sky. The image is masked by a diagonal edged shape covering the right side of the image, which appears to be an element of the architecture, and therefore an internal mask. An irregular hexagon matte supercedes this masking, covering everything but the upper left portion of the image where the building corner meets the sky. The size and shape of this hexagon changes rapidly in two to four frame alternations, which generates an optical illusion of a three-dimensional form alternately inverting as a protruding or hollowed out form. There is also time lapse cloud motion across the sky area.

5. A balcony corner with a brightly lit wall and floor, with sea and sky in the distance. Leaves and paper are blown about the balcony space. The white horizontal line of the wall acts as another internal matte, but all elements of the architecture, sky and ocean shift as the light and exposure varies so that at times the horizon between sky and ocean is indistinguishable.

6. A return to the same profilmic space as in part one, this time framed by a double matte consisting of a black rectangle in the center and a black border around the image, so that the only visible area of image is a picture frame shape. The mattes and image exposed change in size.

Striped shadows within the image from diagonals, so that the stripes
of light and shadow in the various colors (bright red, white, various
shades in shadow) form abstract patterns that dominate over the
recognition of objects.

We can understand these six sections of the film as each involved in the
performances of illusions, a visual play of ambiguity marked by a generalized
indecidability and fluctuation of spatial representation. At moments the
architecture and still-life matter is delineated with the textural precision of
hyper-realism, but the image, once fragmented and reframed by mattes, is
reformulated as abstract compositional elements, modulated arrangements of
changing color and light.

The shifting of elements within the image (the shaking of leaves on the
trees, the movements of light and shadow, the waving curtains) in the fast
motion rendering appear as "artificial" motions. Here the disturbance of
representation, of the normal temporality of motion associated with these
objects, acts similarly to the impossible spatial representations of the sculpture
boxes mentioned earlier; the clouds in section 4, rendered in time lapse look
like animated cut-outs, like the cardboard "clouds" hung in the diorama
representations. These illusions take the codes that comprise the illusion of
reality as a point of departure; their functioning is dependent on a restructuring
of those codes of spatial and temporal representation. This point deserves
emphasis in light of an ideological critique which would define the avant-garde
project as "anti-illusionist."[9] These studies of filmic illusion do not have the
same ideological function as films in which the illusion of reality serves to
support audience belief in the ideological representations contained in a
fiction. Instead, they present filmic illusions in the most straightforward
manner as enticements to visual play and as invitations to analyze these
mechanisms of visual fascination.

In this regard it is interesting to go back to the title of the film as suggesting
a notion of light and shape with a punning reference to erogeneity. The film
releases the eroticism of surfaces, both the surfaces of the represented objects
and the surface of projected light on the screen. It is an eroticism removed from
standard erotic representation, one which has shifted to a focussing of libidinal
energy on a luminous zone in which a multi-leveled modulation is orchestrated.
This is evidenced in the abstract patterns of rhythm throughout the film. There
is an overall "jiggling" of the image in addition to the changing image sizes,
changing spatial relationships, changes in degrees of abstraction or
representational recognizability, changes in light and color, and the movement
of objects within the representation. Through the organization and variation of
these rhythmic pulsings and changing patterns, the film engages us in a
temporal aspect of fascination, which can be understood psychoanalytically as
linked to the most basic formative experiences of perception and cognition,

and in particular to the subject's mastering of change understood as loss in what Freud analyzed as the "fort-da" game in *Beyond the Pleasure Principle*.[10] The child's repetitious play gives him or her power over the threatening situation of absence. Repetition becomes a source of pleasure, but finds its negative manifestation in the potentially self-destructive compulsion to repeat. Art, in its manipulation of abstract patterns, has the potential for emphasizing repetition, variation or a more anarchistic random ordering. A film like *Luminous Zone* raises questions concerning how the formal inscription of such patterning can be discussed ideologically. As elements of the visual image are alternated in patterns in each of the six sections, we can see that all three principles of ordering come into play; rhythms are repeated, but also varied, and randomness is introduced in the irregularities of changing from one pattern to another. However, the beginning and closing segments of the film involve the same figuration of objects, colors and shapes, and the matting patterns are reversals of each other (rectangles framing the image, then the image a frame within the matte rectangles). This gives the form of the film a structural logic similar to that found in the classic narrative film, where opening and closure are defined by rhyming reversal patterns. Like the reversal patterns in *Translucent Appearances,* these effects suggest a complex form of visual articulation in which subtle visual occurrences are explored through the restriction of certain aspects of expression. Repetition and variation become another frame through which we see, a device for emphasizing what might be overlooked.

We can then come to understand the films as proposing a visual ideology of pleasure to be derived from increased attention to perception and the exploration of visual illusions and formal patterning within a temporal frame. The connection of that pleasure to a referent in the world is suggested only to objects, surfaces, motion and light; it is a pleasure most directly linked to the screen image, the area of projected light. In a culture which has come to love the watching of this zone, but primarily considers (either critically or naively) the references contained in the representations which pass through it, these films present that love, that pleasure in a highly abstract and therefore emphatic form. One can consider the relationship of Gerson's films to the skillfully constructed classic film as comparable to the relationship between recent canvases of De Kooning and the paintings of Van Gogh—the abstraction magnifies and isolates the expressivity which earlier was part of a system of representational signification.

Another solution to the construction of films to explore the subtle transformations of light and color is evidenced in the film work of Larry Gottheim. Gottheim's early work relies on the development of a visual action. This action may be as subtle as the changing light or atmosphere in an environment, or it may be caused by camera motion and reframing. Those of

Gottheim's films that I will discuss in this chapter retain concerns with the referentially inscribed landscape or still life to a far greater degree than occurs in Gerson's films. They also insist on an integral view of the visual action, either by consisting only of a single shot or by being a series of one shot takes, as in *Barn Rushes*. This is not to suggest, however, that the viewed phenomena are transparently seen through the film; rather, the film mechanisms (which are variously brought into play in each of the films) determine selection of the visual actions and their transformation into images. As a result we become aware of watching the gradual modification of an image in time and through motion.

Gottheim's *Fog Line* serves as a good example of this process. The eleven-minute film consists of a single fixed shot on a valley meadow, the view of which is nearly obscured at first by a dense fog. The progression of time in the film is marked by the gradual, steady "lifting" of this fog. The change of atmosphere provokes an equally gradual and steady transformation of many of the attributes of the image. As the fog becomes gradually less dense, the opaque white initial image which lent emphasis to the grainy texture of the film-stock, slowly gains more green hue, yet the color system remains relatively monochromatic (ranging from white through progressively more vivid tints of green). Coupled with this is the increasingly greater resolution within the image (caused not by lens adjustments, but by the lessening of the fog), which allows for the emergence of vague shapes that become increasingly distinct outlines of recognizable objects. These objects include two lines (possibly telephone wires or power lines) which traverse the image in the foreground at a nearly horizontal diagonal, and trees and animals which become visible in the depth of the image. This very sense of depth is only gradually realized, as the initial white image appears quite flat and abstract. Only through the change of light and atmosphere within the profilmic space is spatial depth in the image acquired and iconic recognition made possible. There is much in the visual experience of *Fog Line* which compares to Gerson's *Metamorphosis,* except that in Gottheim's film the camera apparatus is fixed not only physically, but remains fixed in all possible adjustments, including focus (the variable in *Metamorphosis*); the film's dynamics can be understood as the registration of exterior variables by a fixed mechanism. Like Andy Warhol's *Empire, Fog Line* develops a concept of film as a framed image, determined by the fixing of a camera position, the choice of a film stock (which in the case of *Fog Line* renders soft color) and duration, marked by gradually unfolding changes in the graphic qualities of that image.

This framing of a slow filmic gesture in *Fog Line* creates a figural space. The obscured visibility makes the distant movements of the animals and the flight of a bird across the image obtain the quality of a memory vision in the same way symbolist painting used soft lines and misty representations to suggest apparitions rather than representations of corporal reality. Thus vision is given as the evocation of memory traces; vision and memory are linked. This linkage becomes an aspect of the force of the film, as there is an element of the uncanny in seeing what appears to be a memory. The slow pace of change which borders on stasis accentuates this sense of the uncanny, as the rhythm of the film itself creates a temporal suspension.

Gottheim has written about those of his films which share the conceptual frame of *Fog Line*'s single shot construction in a manner, although looser and more general in its terminology, that is still thoroughly compatible with the theoretical concepts I have been developing:

> In each case, played off these external divisions that are the same for each viewer are those inner events which vary somewhat from viewing to viewing; the region where something is noticed, is realized. Attention is directed outward at the screen charged with potentiality, and at the same time one is listening inside to one's own experiencing.
>
> There is a performance element in these films (beyond the actual performing of the acts within them, in *Blues* and *Corn*): I mean the unrolling of the film span itself, the feat of catching attention and holding it in pleasurable tension until the very end.[11]

Note Gottheim's emphasis on "inner events," on a "screen *charged* with *potentiality*," on "pleasurable tension." While these phrases contain elements of a phenomenological view of subjectivity outside of the concerns of a libidinal economy, they also suggest a concern with an affective force. The films are constructed (through the fixity of the camera apparatus and the insistence on duration of a single image) to situate a viewer so that visual traces are framed, extended, expanded, to magnify these traces, enlarging them to the dimensions of a spectacle. This formal operation needn't be limited to a formal analysis; it suggests the imaginary activity inherent in viewing an image. Through the use of such devices, the film image refuses to be locked into a metaphorical interpretation which converts the image into fixed signifieds.

This is perhaps most clearly seen as regards Gottheim's films *Blues* and *Corn*. The route of formal reduction would treat the films as insistent on the singular (one subject, the shot, one completed action) and would perhaps place this minimalism in the history of film as a pointed joke. The reflexive, metaphorical reading would constitute the minimal film as the bearer of a clear and singular signification, as in this example written by Scott McDonald:

> Gottheim does more, however, than present an everyday reality in a subtle and beautiful way. In all of his minimal films Gottheim creates a visual strategy similar to the literary device of "synecdoche," a metaphor in which a part represents the whole. In *Blues* the rhythmic elimination of the berries and the emergence of the milk is a two-sided metaphor which suggests that if we concentrate, we will not only improve our lives by enjoying the fruits of the earth more fully, but will be able to move beyond our perception of everyday realities into a more powerful and more fundamental illumination, a level of experience which transcends physical reality itself.
>
> Gottheim also draws attention to the process of film through his use of film texture as a

noticeable component of his image, through his decision to include the "overexposed" tail of
the roll of film and, more subtly, by using the patterns which create the rhythmic harmony of
the film as metaphors for aspects of the film experience. This is most evident in the regular
appearance of more or less still images, each slightly changes: a perfect metaphor for the way
in which film frames usually function. [12]

A close look at the films will indicate why such critical strategies are insufficient
(and in their totalizing claims for the primacy of an insufficient explanation,
wrong).

Blues, although limited to one shot and "stripped down" in its mise-en-
scène, is a complex, active film. The image is of a turquoise-toned pottery bowl,
glazed with white patterns on a surface covered with turquoise a tone deeper
than the bowl. In the bowl float blueberries of various colors in the blue to
violet range. This still life is brightly lit by sunlight which is so intense as to
appear as artificial, highly directional lighting casting sharply defined deep
shadows and raising equally sharply defined highlights in the blueberries and
bowl. A spoon intrudes from the left of the frame to remove some blueberries
only to disappear and repeat this action at intervals until all the blueberries
have disappeared. Each intrusion upsets the composition of the berries, as a
random action, reordering the remaining berries. There is often a delayed
reaction of movement and repositioning after the spoon has been retracted.
Blues insists on the creative gesture implicit in the recording of a controlled
chance occurrence and of repeated modifications as does much conceptual art
and music. But the concerns are not here limited to the conceptual; seemingly
trivial objects are given consideration by play on the visual form of the pottery
bowl (turquoise toned to white swirls, movements of tones of blues) being
extended to the objects surrounding the bowl. The action exists as a frame for a
series of visual events; the orange toned flares at beginning and end are double
markers of the initiation and completion of action and/ or the roll of film being
used. The series of events can be delineated as: (1) depletion of berries; and (2)
regular rhythmic interventions (the spoon) which produce an active visual
change and introduce chance rearrangements of the composition (the berries),
followed by a return to compositional stasis, repeated, until a final stasis is
achieved. And yet there is another consistent, continual pulsing of light
(brighter/ dimmer, in alternation) throughout the film. It becomes more
noticeable, however, after the berries are gone, when only the white milk forms
a blank screen within the image to reflect this light effect.

We can thus see *Blues* as a complex object exploring artistic form (still life
composition and the opening, duration and completion of action) and random
and improvisational movement within that form. "Blues" becomes a doubly
suggestive name for the film by reference both to the monochromatics of the
composition and the punning reference to the musical form which shares this
concern with an established form affected by improvisations.

What is particularly disturbing about McDonald's approach is that the functions it claims to uncover are the most hackneyed formulas for the functioning of art, which read as moral lessons in transcendentalism: concentration will move us to greater fulfillment and perception of reality will lead us to a level of experience which transcends physical reality. Does every instance of a static image, containing slight changes, delight us only because of its perfection as a metaphor for the structure of projected celluloid?

We must learn how to speak of these films in ways that don't limit their evocative plurality. There are always new ideas emerging from each repeated viewing, but it also is necessary to maintain a cautionary discretion in establishing the field of meanings. Given this precaution, I would like to suggest another way to speak of *Blues* which involves its mise-en-scène of food. I am concerned here not with an interpretation of the imagery, but rather how the framing and representation of the image of food operates in relationship to visual drives, and serves to comment on this operation.

Although *Blues* was in fact shot with an extreme telephoto lens from some height above, the resultant image is a close-up high angle looking down into the bowl, similar to the subjective view of someone seated at a table looking down into food placed before her or him. Of course, this subjective placement is modified by the extreme lighting and the artificiality of the sideways entrance of the spoon into the image. Yet even with this extremely forced coding of subjectivity, one is reminded of similar "realistic" efforts in two Hollywood films, *Lady in the Lake* and *Dark Passage,* in which the extended use of subjective angles is tied to a first person point-of-view narration with which the audience is led to identify. These films court the danger of forced contrivance in the mise-en-scène of such events as tying one's shoes; the spectator can no longer "identify" with the hands entering the frame. Rather than labeling *Blues* as the same kind of imaginary placement of the viewer in the scene, seated above the bowl, looking down at the results of his (imaginary) eating, let us say instead that the image's reference to that placement is more ironic and reflective than such images in a narrative context. The scene, choreographed for this special close-up performance, remains a visual composition posited as an image series.

This dichotomy points, however, to an intriguing psychoanalytic relationship between the mouth and eye, a relationship with which this film teasingly plays. Robert Fleiss speaks of an "eye-mouth unit" as facilitating primary identification, in which the oral-sadistic activity of an infant is replaced by a visual "taking in." Fleiss is led to amend Freud's remarks on scopophilia as a result of this new theory, as follows:

> The tactile pleasure, replaced by the pleasure in seeing is that accompanying the tactile cognizance, originally achieved by the mouth into which the small infant is apt to put anything within reach as if in order to know it. One might say that a little later, when the

motor mastery requisite to coordination renders the objects three-dimensional and thereby, perhaps, provocative of ocular incorporation, he "put" everything "into" his eyes. And one may regard the unblinking gaze of the infant as indicative of the eye's imitating the mouth of the first oral phase before imitating that of the second. The hand gradually supplements the percept gained by the eye, whose motor contribution, e.g., to the sublimated aesthetic enjoyment of the adult, has not always found proper appreciation. It is in this motor function of the unit of mouth and eye that the much discussed "empathic consummation of art" has its origin; and it is here that the name "taste" for aesthetic discrimination—a name that derives from "ME. *tasten* to feel, fr. OF. *taster,* to try by the touch (Webster)—finds its justification.[13]

Blues can thus be seen as involving a visual pun on the lofty critical cliché, "a feast for the eyes." But the humor here seriously evokes the subject's libidinal relationship to the image surface, and the possibility of a satisfaction of libidinal drives in the aesthetic experience of artistic seeing. The difference between the theory of libidinal economy and Fleiss's theory is that Fleiss still uses the phrase "sublimated aesthetic enjoyment of the adult" which, in its common acceptance has come to mean a simple, singular, and established transfer of sexual (base) energy to aesthetic (elevated) energy. Aesthetic enjoyment is not seen as an active, ongoing energetic process occurring unconsciously. It is generally understood as an already completed and sealed transfer, a notion already somewhat present in Freud's definition: "the sexual instinct places extraordinarily large amounts of force at the disposal of civilized activity, and it does this in virtue of being able to displace its aim without materially diminishing its intensity. This capacity to exchange its originally sexual aim for another one which is no longer sexual but is psychically related to the first aim, is called the capacity for sublimation."[14] Freud structures his definition around aims rather than the transfer and circulation of drives. Subsequently sublimation has accrued a more static interpretation than a theory defined by drives.

Lyotard avoids use of the term "sublimation," speaking instead of a direct libidinal current established between object and viewer. Once we shift the focus back to the economic processes of energetic circulation (notions elsewhere suggested in Freud's own work) each creative activity (viewing art, as well as producing it) evokes a specific circulation of that energy.

Thus, even though *Corn* is somewhat similar to *Blues,* there is a considerable difference in its functioning in this regard. *Corn* begins with another still-life framing, this time a medium shot on a wooden counter top that extends diagonally from upper left to lower center of the image. A brown-toned ceramic bowl is placed in the center of this wooden platform. This portion of the image is brightly lit, but the area comprising the right half of the image adjoining this diagonal is engulfed in total darkness. This constitutes the counter as a kind of stage and the dark area as the "wings," an effect which becomes more pronounced as hands emerge from darkness, briefly as an almost unrecognizable blur, to drop corn husks in the area behind the bowl. The mysterious puppeteer manipulates the performers with intervals of presence and disappearance, similar to the activity of the spoon in *Blues,* but here, instead of evacuating elements of the viewed object, the manipulations build a sculptural form as the striated green husks and gold and brown silk pile up into a sensual mass of color and texture. Each addition modifies the form both by adding to its shape and by causing movements in the rest of the pile, movements which sometimes continue as a subtle shifting long after the hand has been retracted. Then there is a long period in which no more intruding action occurs from the "wings" and the only change in an otherwise fixed image is in the sunlight which gradually shifts in color and shape, at times affecting the reflected highlights on the corn husk form. Then a corn holder drops cooked and steaming ears of corn into the frame, piling them as a second sculptural structure in the bowl. In contrast to the random scattering of husks, the ears of corn are piled into neat rows, a composition emphasized by the rows of kernels, creating a light and shadow perspective angling backwards in the frame paralleling the counter due to the placement of some of the ears to create this angle. The corn glows in the bright sunlight and shimmers as the heat affects the atmosphere around it. Especially remarkable as the visual trace of this heat energy is the vapor rising above the corn causing wavering distortions in the husk pile seen through this mobile filter. The film holds again on the now-filled bowl in still life composition as the light continues to change shape, retracting until the film's end.

Instead of framing and actions which would emphasize the comparison between aesthetic viewing of an art object and the drives and pleasure associated with the consumption of food, *Corn* presents the process of food preparation as an elaborate dramatic action, performed on an intensely lit stage, but also elided from vision in the dark recesses of the wings and offscreen space. During the cooking process that comprises the middle of the film, an almost static composition is the continual marker of an absence, of the unseen and the nonindicated.

We can think of the film as a micro-narrative, the telling of one discrete action composed of a simple series of functions. There is a sole gesture of narrative opening (the corn is stripped and readied for cooking), but there is no sustaining function of the action, either seen, heard or otherwise indicated. The middle action is missing, but the film has a middle; suddenly the object of the narration is pulled off through a black shadow in the image and then reappears, altered in form to close the narrative. Untold, this action of cooking still remains placed within the narrative. *Corn* explores the relation between modes of expressive transformation and film narration. The manipulation of time and space within film marrative and the use of the borders of the image frame differ drastically in *Corn* from ellipsis and offscreen narrative occurrences in classic films, as well as those whose expansion of these categories have aroused so much critical and theoretical attention (films by Renoir, Bresson, Dreyer, Duras, and Straub/Huillet, among others). What differentiates Gottheim's work in this film? The answer is to be found in a combination of the following factors: absence of sound indicators, the absence of personalized human agents, the static fixity of the image during the offscreen action, the reduction of the entire representation and narrative to actions performed on objects that even so maintain a theatricality. These qualities combine within the film to create a perplexing interrogation of the status of action and narration within the cinematic image. How deep has our learned cognizance of offscreen action become that we imagine it even when it isn't indicated? How do we react to that block of "dead" screen time when the narrative suspends itself in ellipsis and we are left watching an image? How do the processes of transformation (both the visual ones which are seen and the major narrative one which isn't) relate to the final still-life composition, which visually reminds us in composition and lighting of the still-life tradition in painting? Partial, incomplete, fragmented moments, so outside the tradition of the perfect full and plentiful still-life composition and an attention to process establish this film as different than other (classic, modernist) modes of film making and from easel/gallery art. By structuring its duration as a process of change, by doubly implicating narrative as paradoxically at once inside and outside the image, and by imbedding these rather sophisticated theoretical questions in the apparent banality of an everyday operation of cooking corn, the film accomplishes that multi-leveled fascination which comes to characterize the films included in this chapter. Seemingly so simple, so lacking in the conventional notions of significant, expressed meaning, these films play with the transformation of images to investigate a theory of force and meaning. Operations on representation evoke the history of figural and narrative art, but these films' images, in their difference from those traditions, expose what is habitually unseen in the act of seeing.

Gottheim's later works move away from the conceptual framework of gradual transformations to a more complex functioning of differences across repetition in both sound and image (and their interaction). The more recent films tend to take on concerns which join those of the films discussed in the next chapter. *Barn Rushes* and *Harmonica,* though, can be seen as transitional films; they maintain the restricted frame, while developing complex rhythmic articulations in the case of *Barn Rushes* and a tension between mimetic and nonmimetic functions in *Harmonica.*

Barn Rushes is composed of a series of similar camera movements (a tracking movement left from a vehicle simultaneous with a pan right) past the same field of view, dominated by an old, weathered barn whose missing slats create a complex filter and mask for the light shining behind it. The barn is the constant, always in the frame, and the camerawork is a continual recentering. This does not mean that the barn is always centered; rather, the barn drifts toward either frame edge, continually shifting position. This play with repositioning occurs relative to background (the barn and field) and foreground space (the reeds and rushes) as well, due to the converse force of the tracking movement with its internally changing angles. Each camera movement to the left is a separate take (the duration of one spring wind) marked as such by the flares at beginning and end. These takes are grouped into eight sections, each section containing an internal orchestration of light, atmosphere, framing effects and changes in color, (particularly noticeable as vivid changes in the sky). An interesting analysis of this camera movement has been offered by Morgan Fisher:

> It is significant to me that the geometry of the shot is radial. It is as if the shot is legitimized by being the opposite of the pan, that reflex that Eastman Kodak warns all amateurs against excessive use of. To extend the use of a term found in mathematics, particularly in the study of polytopes and projective geometry, the shot is the *dual* of a pan. In a pan the camera turns on a fixed point that corresponds to the center of a circle, while the lens is directed along a radius that sweeps the circle's circumference. In *Barn Rushes* this relation is reversed. It is the camera that occupies the edge, travelling along the periphery while aimed at a subject that occupies the fixed center. Instead of extending a point into a line, the shot compresses a line into a point. In both cases, however, the camera is aimed along a radius: in a pan, outward; in *Barn Rushes,* inward.[15]

The visual consequence of this movement is a shimmering light and blurring of part of the image, so that the background and foreground appear to be in discrepancy. While one part is clearly focussed, the other blends into the dots and slashes associated with the impressionist canvas (an effect available to the eye trained on fields from a speeding car). The theoretical consequence is already inherent in Fisher's term, "turning inward." Like *Translucent Appearances,* we have an almost obsessive reiteration of relationships (graphic, light) but each inscription is distinctly different, original and functioning in a reverberating relationship to the others. Each take participates in the temporal repetition of a series of effects affecting the psychophysiology of the viewer; one is caught, taken up, affected, by a vibrant, ecstatic rushing movement.

Energetic activity is differently treated in *Harmonica,* which is at once a more humorous and intellectual film, although the overwhelming sensuousness is not lost with the increased attention to these other dimensions. Here again is the single shot with a fixed frame, but the shot is within a moving car shooting across the back seat, in which a harmonica player actively gestures and bounces through the frame as he plays, and an open car door window frames the autumn colors of a wooded countryside in muted focus.

The game that ensues involves the represented correlation of and imaginary relationship between sound and image track. At the film's start, when the harmonica player plays, the synchronized sound operates in full mimesis, creating a naturalistic correspondence between movement (the player's exaggerated gestures of lips, hand, body), air and sound. This gives way to another type of gesture, as the player thrusts his harmonica in and out of the window, turning it in the wind, depicted on the sound track by a corresponding single chord emitted when the wind "blows" the harmonica. The representation is a literal representation of Coleridge's extended metaphor in "The Eolian Harp," changed by extension in time (the film lasts 10 ½ minutes) and a fascinating play with the border between mimetic realism/ representation of fantasy. Gesture, movement and air are suggested causes of sound in the image, which leads us to wonder about the relation of a sound track to a "causal" image track; across the film, the artificial and fantasy aspects of such correspondence become more intriguing than referential or metaphoric readings of the scene. This is a film framing nature, putting it into a filmic placement where artifice gains its own interest; we see through a moving open window frame, we hear through the audacious manipulation of sound synced to visual gesture. The film pushes the Eolian harp away from the pantheistic celebration towards a greater sensitivity to the mechanics of a pleasurable apparatus where "a light in sound, a sound like power in light, rhythm in all thought, and joyance everywhere" is the evocative force generated by the film itself.

5

Visual Dynamics, Referential Tensions and Conceptual Film

A flamboyant rage of color and light swirl across the screen; in this rushing, dynamic activity, fragments of representation remain. Representation, even fragmented, establishes the possibility of complex referential coding. In addition to these hints at a referential coding, possible signifieds, there is a verbal title which suggests another reference, another way of indicating meaning. Yet the accentuated dynamics seem to overpower and act against the signified, the represented within the images.

I have outlined here a type of film organized to create disjunction, a separation of the functioning of visual dynamics and representational coding. This disjunction creates a tension which undercuts interpretations the inscribed reference would have in another context.

Just as with the films of gradual transformations discussed in the last chapter, these films of elaborate, rapid changes, of more complex and articulated structures, create a problematic interaction between force and signification which brings attention to force. The enjoyment of this energy expenditure can best be discussed in the terms Lyotard has suggested in "L'Acinéma"[1] (as I indicated in chapter 2). The metaphor of pyrotechniques is used to present the pleasure derived from releases of energy which are nonproductive, nonutilitarian. Lyotard points to the psychoanalytic foundation of such pleasure in reference to Freud's discussion of orgasm in *Beyond the Pleasure Principle* as a conjunction of life and death instincts.[2]

While I agree with Lyotard's assessment of the pleasure mechanisms involved and will speak to the specifics of explosive eruptions of energy through light and color variation in the specific films, I want to investigate further how this force operates relative to the codes of representation in the images and then to explore how this operation, through disjunction, engenders new meanings for the films. It is at this level that the films serve as interrogations of signifying processes, in that they make problematic the referential functions of the image. The visual outline of an object can be submitted to various manipulations so that it becomes a site of visual contrasts and dynamics which no longer have anything to do with the object. Our analysis will determine how this disjunction signifies, and what meanings it suggests.

Since the analysis of these films will lead to a discussion of problems of referentiality and signifying practices in avant-garde films, I will then examine some films which approach these same questions differently; I will end the chapter with a discussion of some films whose functioning is tied to that of conceptual art. As such, they function as apparent opposites to the films that dominate the first part of the chapter; they restrict expressive uses of film techniques in order to concentrate on conceptual relations between art and language, image and meaning. The question is, do these films evacuate the expressive aspects of the image? Changes of light, color, rhythms and disjunctive operations in abstraction/representation and image/sound relationships are still very much at play in this supposedly "conceptual" filmmaking practice. The network of interaction between force and signification is as involved as in the previously discussed films, but in this second instance the images' expressive qualities, instead of being presented as an obvious central concern, enter into the referential system of meaning as a marked surplus. The nature of this "marking" is to designate the inescapability of expression within the filmic image.

The works of Hollis Frampton will dominate the chapter, since his films display both of these opposing tendencies. Many of his films are constructed with sweeping gestures, rapid changes either in editing or camerawork. The rhythm is an engulfing, active, powerful onslaught of change, of differences, causing a vibrant surface of projection displaying extremes of contrast and fluctuation. Yet these films are placed beside conceptual films which apparently counteract the expressive filmic surface, grouped together within a larger corpus, to which Frampton has given the name, "The Magellan Cycle."

A metaphor of navigation, of crossing time zones, of exploration, Magellan serves Frampton's ambition to open the epic thematics in film which have been the province of literature as various as Homer, Proust and Joyce, without using narrative codes to reproduce the representational film mode of classic or modernist cinema. Instead the exploration of these thematic questions emerges from juxtapositions of images and sometimes sounds outside a narrative form. Yet Magellan's name is given to this striving, and Frampton will speak of "a fictional biography of a protagonist,"[3] choosing an external, metaphorical reference to which this disparate filmic exploration is said to cohere.

The metaphor remains, however, extremely loose, never directly represented in the films, but its literary foundations (the epic, the rhetorical figures of poetry) are joined in some of the films by literary and linguistic concerns, as the sound track and written matter in the image manipulate language. And even in the films in which silence accompanies a flow of semi-abstracted images, the name of the film often pulls it into place within the cycle, so that the metaphor covers and connects the various separate film parts. One way to consider the cycle is to think of it as Frampton's critical elaboration on his own films; he not only creates an ensemble out of heterogeneous assortment of films, but suggests elaborate groupings and sub-groupings, therefore channeling the diversity into a more controlled interpretive grid. Coupled with this global metaphorical naming is Frampton's fantasy of a projection that would be spread out over a year and a day in short segments. This fantasy to build a cathedral out of the films, a massive environment which one periodically and religiously visits, seems far removed from the reflexive, materialist gesture supposedly assigned the avant-garde. Instead we must confront the force of the obsession, as expressed through the images, color and camera movements which haunt one through their internal recurrence in a film and their reemergence from film to film. Symmetries, reversals, contradictions, unity and disjunction all enter into the picture, weave through the complex.

Hollis Frampton's *The Gates of Death* is an example of a nonverbal filmic expression which nonetheless encompasses the mythic project described above. It develops paradigmatic oppositions and thematization similar to those which have been historically associated with literature.

The film is composed of camera movements, sweeping close-up pans, over and around the surfaces of dissected parts of human bodies whose tissue and bones have been preserved in a state of arrested decay, mummification. These images occur in black and white, but are also seen with overlaid surfaces of color, one of reds and yellows, one of greens and yellows. These layers of color echo the color used in the brief, repeated inserts of similar swaying, panning motions over hexagonal tiles. The tile imagery is superimposed upon itself, appearing as highly abstracted cell-like images. Exposition of iconic filmic material and the abstract punctuation of that material thus become entwined due to the similar rhythmic camera movements and superimpositions.

Repetition plays a major role in the presentation of the iconic material. There are a limited number of different shots, including: (1) the panning across a skull cut in half, open to display as mirrored symmetrical halves of complex structures; (2) a face which looks like a Chinese mask; (3) a head pointed downward in the frame with a slit in the neck; (4) a woman's face with an eye and the nose missing, giving it the appearance of a smashed china doll; (5) a close-up of toes, and many images of fragments of bodies which puzzle the viewer attempting to participate in a game of recognition. These images are repeated, sometimes reversed and inverted, sometimes colored, sometimes superimposed over the reversal of themselves.

This repetition/variation pattern of unfolding has obvious effects in creating rhythms. But further, all these echoing fragments of an emerging global rhythm acquire an added significance as they engender a feeling of ceremony, a ritual for the eyes, the substance of which is the exploration of cavities, protrusions, and landscapes of human bodies. As such the visual exploration gains a highly eroticized charge, one that is potentially disturbing (perhaps a source of "displeasure" for many viewers responding to that eroticism with denial), due to the fact that the bodies are dead. The details of the representation of the bodies continually confront us with death, the degeneration of flesh, the physical sight of mortality.

The impact of these images can be understood in reference to the deeply constituted psycho-social taboos which these images evoke. The foundations of the taboo are suggested by Georges Bataille in his book, *Eroticism* as being linked to "the contagion of violence."[4] The cadaver is a sign of violence which then creates in it the menacing possibility of further violence. Bataille cites Freud's remarks in *Totem and Taboo*[5] concerning the taboo on touching and on naming the dead in primitive societies. This taboo grows out of a fear of the dead's demonic power, what Freud calls a projection of the survivor's own ambivalence towards the deceased. However, Bataille wishes to extend the scope of his comments beyond the tribal and familial context of Freud's inquiry to ask why the cadaver as such (even, as in the case of Frampton's film, anonymous corpses) continues to terrify. So besides seeing the cadaver as a sign of violence, Bataille also calls it a "sign of less than nothing, worse than nothing."[6]

This concept of the figuration of nothingness in the image of the corpse raises in a new and intriguing manner the problem of force and signification. No longer are we in a realm of composition bordering on the nonfigurative and yet we still approach a kind of death, a silence of signification, in the image of death. "To signify less than nothing" is to signify the fear of the force of the lack of signification. Narrative images for the most part contain a circulation of human bodies, which even when depicted in static framings are caught in the midst of actions. These images in *The Gates of Death* present dead and decaying bodies which are sometimes difficult to recognize as traces of once living humans, but the camera circulates around these less than human object/remains, creating activity, movement. The paradigmatic oppositions life/death, active/passive, erotic/morbid, seen/hidden are transgressed by the structuration of the film. The audience is forced to touch again and again, with its eyes, the untouchable dead flesh. The fascination in which the audience is invited to participate, (given that the lighting and framing of the images, the lyric sweeping camera, the rhythms of the returns create an aesthetic experience out of this visual examination) is thus of a sexual nature; this is not so much a film of horror before death, but an extended fascination with its traces, a visual ritual of necrophilia.

The dynamics are that of reversability, a repeated series of motions in continually changing variations echoing the complex rhythms of a ritual dance. This imagery is infused with vitality, sensuality and pleasure, here where we are least expecting it, or willing to accept its appearance.

These swirling repetitions of movement are characteristic of much of Frampton's film work, so that this film can serve as a model for our analysis. It also *marks* its own reversability (and here we can refer to the notion of the "writerly text" defined by Barthes,[7] as one which can be entered without regard to its "good order," or linearity and development from beginning to end) by giving us not only repetitions and reprises of images, but also their occasional presentation upside down, in superimposition with a reversed (left to right) version of themselves or with different colors. The fragments of bodies float in space as they float in our memories, turning and returning, lacking the order of discourse, escaping through reversability into another figural space, one which retains a charged referentiality, an iconicity.

Transformation of associations we might normally make with the iconic material in question is displayed in three films which are grouped by Frampton as *Summer Solstice, Autumnal Equinox* and *Winter Solstice*. These titles evoke special days in the navigation of the year, days of seasonal change that are associated with ancient celebrations, based on an early recognition of solar cycles. Each of the films is composed of homogeneous iconic material which differs greatly from film to film, yet the camera movements in all cases are similar, graceful, yet sometimes abrupt. Combinations of pans and tilts, often in distinct "L" shapes, explore an object or process, but occasionally appear to be an almost arbitrary slashing out of a fragment of visual space, an autonomous act unconcerned with complementing the representational aspects of the objects or actions appearing in the image.

Given this similarity, three very distinct films emerge differing both in referential coding and compositional distinctions. *Summer Solstice* is shot in a cow pasture so that the frames are mostly composed of the close-up images of black and white markings on the cow hides and the shapes formed by parts of their bodies, set against the vivid green of the space which surrounds them. Here the camera framings and movements seem an imposition on an imaginary coded vision of the pastoral scene, that is, one which would respect a notion of the pastoral, of tranquility. This imaginary image could consist of a static framing or slow, gradual movement, isomorphic to and respectful of the "natural atmsophere" surrounding these cows in a world outside this image. Instead, *Summer Solstice* violates that image through a turbulence of motion, contrast, activity. The cinematic rendering is in conflict with a given level of referential reading of the image. The idyllic, romantic potential that is expressed in a film like Brakhage's *Troegoedia*, a lyrical filmic celebration of the movements of goats, here is abandoned in favor of an explosive dynamism which cannot be traced back to a vision of nature, or a subjective vision before the natural. The disjunction is one not only of art and nature, but also of technology (the cinematic apparatus) and nature, a process comparable to that operative in Bette Gordon's film *Still-Life* where images of cows are submitted to various manipulations of exposure and coloration within the refilmed, repeated image.

This active and disjunctive imposition of technology is a strong statement delineating a contemporary direction for art which has ideological consequences. One is confronted with a pleasure not grounded in representation, meaning, the reconstitution through art of man's place in nature or his subjective individuality in the world. The artwork will not so meditate, ideologically, nor cover its visual fascination with a weave of signifieds. Dynamic expressivity is exposed and opened to intense enjoyment, the referential is used against its culturally determined signifieds.

In *Autumnal Equinox*, the scene which is carved into expressive fragments is the interior of a modern slaughter house. Due to the activity of the cattle being butchered, carcasses being hacked into cuts of meat, blood flowing as pools of reflected light, the fragmentation and movement is seen here to expressively correspond to the referential scene. Yet the disjunction here is again related to the rendering of these acts as a seductive visual experience; in the context of the expressive economy of the film, the violence of slaughter is explored for its visual impact, positively. A scene which is not normally associated with aesthetic pleasure is opened to such an interpretation by the forceful camera which invades it.

Certainly Rembrandt, Francis Bacon and Soutine established the aesthetic interest in the color and movement to be explored in paintings of the hung carcasses familiar to butcher shops. In viewing the carcasses in these paintings and in this film, one is aware of the representation within the image of carnivorous violence. Just as Cézanne's repeated paintings of three skulls differ in their functioning from his mountains or other still lifes due to referential coding, these films maintain a charged referential system of signification.

By grouping *Summer Solstice* and *Autumnal Equinox* together by their titles as a subgroup in the Magellan cycle, and by further pressing comparisons through the similar camera work and punctuation between shots, Frampton is suggesting a life/death paradigm whose constituent elements are capable of exploding as an expressive force. Just as we were asked by *The Gates of Death* to touch the decaying corpses with our eyes, *Autumnal Equinox* asks us to touch the blood and slaughtered animals; we do not "forget" the object of representation in experiencing that touch. A field of associations and culture enter into the vision of the film, widening the disjunction I spoke of earlier, eliciting an active response to an almost unbearable conflict between that which one might rather not see and that with which one is fascinated in the same images.

In another permutation, *Winter Solstice*, rather than displaying the kinds of disjunctions noted above, contains fragmented images of blast furnaces in a steel mill which fully compliment the expressive economy as the elaborate mise-en-scène of pyrotechnics. But if we go back to Lyotard's definition of pyrotechnics, we find that it is a superfluous explosion, a child playing with matches in amazement at the burst of light. So the disjunction in *Winter*

Solstice is between a process of useful production and the extraction of a pyrotechnic film which is *not* useful (as in documentary, as explanation of an exterior phenomenon), but rather playful. This disjunction would be particularly evident in those whose Marxism would condition their expectations of what a film shot inside a factory should be, and who, as a result, might dismiss the film as decadent in its lack of concern with the ideology of labor relations in steel production. Within the context of expression of force beyond cliched referential expectations, this disjunction has another role, which can be analytically extended into a questioning of Marxist assumptions about meaning and truth. This critical project occupies precisely the same persons (Lyotard, Jean Baudrillard) who have theorized on the relationship between force and signification, play and work, art and discourse.[8]

The images of *Winter Solstice* are a glowing yellow, orange and red, framed internally by the black of machine parts, such as the hanging hook, and marked at times by the silhouettes of the workers. A fountain of sparks, large and full, is repeated numerous times; another shower, smaller, scattered; fire spitting out of a circle; a pouring, dripping cascade of burning points; a quick pan down the bright falling flickerings; a glowing metal bar swinging through the frame. Focus adjustments as well as camera movements further abstract the photographed light into greater moving and shifting dynamics.

Taken together these three films raise difficult theoretical questions. It is easy to see that they share a dynamic functioning traceable to the establishment of disjunctions (although these are variously located). They also share a similar movement and framing of shots and the punctuation of shots by contrasting color leader (red against the black, white and green of *Summer Solstice*, green against the reds of *Autumnal Equinox*, blue against the yellow-orange of *Winter Solstice*). What is harder to get at is how these films challenge theories of image signification. It would be too simple to say the referential is inconsequential; in each case the play with signification and our cultural expectations is precisely and individually important to the functioning of the film. We can see now how the films can alter the theories of image reading discussed in chapter 2. Before these films, we must as critics align ourselves with Serres' bafflement and musings before Carpaccio's *The Two Courtesans*, for the rendering generates ambiguities and fluxes of signification rather than certain signs.

The spectator cannot in these cases merely read signs inscribed in the artwork and thus derive its signification; rather the specificity of the images' rendering disturbs what might be considered its culturally determined reserve of signifieds. Disturbs but does not annihilate, for in the tension between pastoral associations and quick movements, between butchery and flows of rich color pools, between a factory and fireworks, we are subjected to a re-emergence of these referential codes.

These films suggest a reflection on those codes, an interrogation of their existence and their power over our vision. Why do we read what we see through the filter of these preconceived expectations? If the viewing of the image is the reinforcement of an idée-reçu—at best a transfer or modification, but perhaps only a reiteration as emblem—what power can be granted the artwork to affect the complacency of the viewer/interpreter? These three films find their force in the celebration of a filmic rendering which overrides those cultural assumptions, affects the spectator, there where he or she was most fixed as reader of an assumed code.

This manipulation of referential difference is explored differently in films whose various sections remain disjunct entities by virtue of distinct referential material. One example of this is Frampton's short film, *Procession*, which divides into three sections as follows:

1. Close-up on flowers, with an alternative flicker pattern in their coloration (green/red).
2. Close-up on the spotted patterning in black and white on cow hide, with a man walking across the frame at the very end of the section.
3. An orange, curved, shiny surface seen through the distortion of an extreme wide angle lens. Arched movements constituting separate shots are edited together, so that the patterns of arched flow accentuate the bulging surface caused by the distorting lens. As the camera moves, a headlight and blinker waves in and out of the frame, and one becomes aware that the reflected colors are actually reflections on the surface of people who are passing along side what comes to be recognizable (as the camera pulls back at the film's end) as an orange pick-up truck.

There is an attenuated progression from part to part; the high contrast red and green of the flowers is picked up in the black and white patterns, while the man crossing at the end of the second section is picked up in the reflections of the passers-by in the third. An antithematic way to play with referential images, *Procession* exists as three different explorations of color contrasts and various forms of vibrant pulsating within the image. Yet the very nonconjunction of these flowers, these cow hides and this truck surface, the incompatibility and refusal to make sense together, to correspond developmentally, is what gives the film its impact.

We have seen how these films fight to escape a culturally determined fixity through carefully wrought disjunctions. *Mouches Volantes*, a film by Larry Gottheim, departs from those films of his discussed in the last chapter in its move towards investigation of the complex functioning of differences across repetitions in sound and image correlations. It presents another type of departure from referential expectations, and another manner in which disjunction is used to these ends.

The film is composed of seven segments of different images, each section distinct in its edited rhythms and visual material (yet all share common characteristics, flow into the memory and anticipation of each other, a matter I will discuss in detail shortly). These seven segments of equal temporal length are separated from one another by slightly exposed black leader. Each section is seen twice so that the order of repetition is also an order of reversal, a mirroring, a pyramid (12345677654321). The sound track is an alternation of silence and repetitions of the same spoken monologue of Angeline Johnson, recounting her life with singer Blind Willie Johnson. The monologue (actually excerpts from an interview) thus constitutes one narration which speaks of a meeting, a love which leads to marriage, blindness, poverty and death. In its spoken form this narrative escapes clichés of melodrama as the vibrant voicing becomes a portrait of its speaker, a figure drawn from the emotional landscape of her specific cultural experience of Black urban poverty. The richness of voice as narrating expression is the richness behind blues singing; the repeated monologues become not so much a narrative but a spoken song whose changes in pitch, timbre and rhythm seem to vary slightly with each exact repetition.

This difference is in part due to a difference always present in any exact repetition (due to the memories established and the alteration of perception which results from these memories). The coupling of each repetition of the voiced narrative with a new segment of images accentuates these differences. Each of the seven image segments punctuates the monologue, through correspondences or contrasts (image shifts in the middle of a voice phrase, or conversely, image patterns which follow these voice phrases). Obviously, the numerous subdivisions of larger patterns are brought into evidence by these changing correlations of image and sound. One "hears" a laugh, a pause, for the first time the sixth or seventh time the monologue is spoken. The tape whirring past the recorder's head producing an audial beat which was always present each time the monologue occurred becomes more evident and serves to underscore articulations in the image in the last segment. Even without the production knowledge that Gottheim labored over these effects by correlating graphs of patterns in sound and image tracks, one hears and sees the orchestration as an exciting counterpoint, a creative exploration which is traceable at least back to Eisenstein and the famous sound manifesto he authored with Pudovkin and Alexandrov.[9] The segments of image which are projected in silence receive a different kind of attention because they are alternated with segments accompanied by sound and exist in comparison with themselves either previously or retrospectively projected with the monologue accompaniment. Here all the questions of the evocative force of silence (particularly in contrast to sounds) that were discussed in chapter 3 are brought into play.

Yet *Mouches Volantes* must be seen not as a complicated exercise, but as the multidimensional channeling and shifting of forces whose evocative reverberation defies the Cartesian sensibility of a structural experiment. The structure is relatively clear and straightforward; the question is what floats, circulates, is transformed within this structure?

The transformations are indicated by the film's title, the scientific term for the small particles which are seen as they float over the cornea and interpreted as bubbles or flecks floating in the external atmosphere. The eye, in trying to focus on them, must try to center them, but as they are not external objects, they inevitably resist centering as they just float away, off the pupil. This phenomenon is a metaphor for a filmic floating of images before the eyes, images that refuse to be fixed and contained, that instead drift through film frames, disappear, and return. Each segment contains distinct images with dominant figures and tonalities: in one case, black and white images of drifting particles in extreme close-up, flashes on waves, in another, high contrast images of a snowstorm, a family, a mother and child inside watching a child outside and various shots of these inside/outside spaces of performance and watching; in another, images by the sea, the dappling patterns of light and vegetation, etc. Certain qualities float through all the segments no matter how variously treated. Each contains drifting of particles, bees, snow or water and one segment even drifts back and forth in alternations and superimpositions between the comparison of the snow seen through the window and the sea seen through plants. Specific camera effects change so that sometimes a zoom, sometimes flash frames, sometimes focus adjustments provide the modification which further inscribe this activity of shifting and transformation. The narrative of these images is evasive; a family or various of its members circulate through the imagery of all except the first (and final) segment, but these figures drift through the images without explanation, as if the spectator were watching the flashes of someone else's memory. This is a quality the film shares with numerous films of Brakhage, particularly *Dog-Star Man, Scenes from under Childhood*, and *Window Water Baby Moving*. However, in *Mouches Volantes* the recurrence of family imagery is juxtaposed with and contrasted to an equally personal voiced monologue. The two personal histories remain separate, in both social referentiality and medium of expression, at times blending in their evocative force at an abstract level of expressive coincidence, at times competing with each other for space, dominance, attention. As such the personal memory traces represented in the film imagery become drifting particles in a larger expressive structure. One does not focus on them (what was this vacation, or this snow storm) but rather loses the investment in the translation of that representation to a larger flux in which the activity of these images as traces, partial objects of narrative and visual expression determines their place in the overall energetic economy of the film. It is possible to interpret Brakhage's films similarly, but as critical writings on his films as keys to his romantic persona indicate, little in the structure of his films suggests one explore this direction. Due to the structural weave of *Mouches Volantes,* one cannot possibly turn the entire film into a representation of personal vision and memory.

Instead, the film resists fixing the image perceptually and consequently, as in the films of Frampton discussed earlier, fixing the image in a familiar system of signification. "Fixing an image" (a phrase with another meaning in photographic developing, which is not without metaphorical resonances here) can be used to refer to a standard viewing of the image; one fixes its internal dynamics into a reading of its representation. These films, through their accentuation of the dynamics of inscription and structuration of a filmic image chain, break down our tendency to fix images by decoding, translating them into fixed meanings. The signifying processes of these films provoke attention to those operations of disjunction and anaphoric functioning potentially occurring in all filmic practices. Here these operations are highlighted by the specific alterations of image structuration in each film.

Let's turn now to those films which take the opposite tack, investigating a conceptual approach to filmic expression. It is extremely difficult to distill one doctrine that exemplifies this range of conceptual artistic activities; perhaps the most useful source for deriving a set of defining characteristics is a volume entitled, *Six Years: The Dematerialization of the Art Object* which includes writings and conceptual pieces from 1966-72.[10] What emerges is a renunciation of the imagist tradition.

Not only can there be no semblances of narrative fiction or illusionist spatial representation, but conceptual art restricts itself from the appeal of colorist or compositional practices which deflect attention from the investigation of the artwork's relationship to linguistic practices (and here we see a parallel to an early semiotic pronouncement that extra-linguistic systems of signification are only understandable in linguistic modes, that verbal language is a "master" system). As a result of its interest in linguistic propositions conceptual art extends its concerns to areas of knowledge previously considered outside the realm of art, particularly scientific formulations. Conceptual art covers a broader spectrum than "reflexivity" although often, in tracing the relationship between semiotic systems, there is a reflexive gesture that serves to define one or more artistic media or practices.

Hollis Frampton's *Poetic Justice* is a concrete presentation of a conceptual artistic practice in film. It begins with a high angle close-up of a table top with a plant on the left, a stack of white paper in the center and a cup of coffee on the right. Then in the successive shots the pad is replaced by sheets of paper each bearing a verbal description of a shot. The film is subdivided as four "tableaux" each marked by a page labeling it. The film being described verbally has characters ("you," "your lover," the filmmaker as "me") and a narrative which includes lovemaking and filming. Due to the descriptions one can, from the words, "visualize" the spatial order and narrative events of the film, but the description refers to the reflexive image being seen, (the conceptual film composed of these shots of pages being placed on the table). The table is described verbally, and the pages echoed by photographs said to be placed on it, as the written matter from shots 2-8 indicate:

#2 Title: *First Tableau*

#3 (long shot) A blooming lilac in early light. scene brightens slowly (slow dissolve to)

#4 (middle shot) Room interior open window. A lilac is seen outside (zoom in and drop to)

#5 (close-up) My hand places a black and white photograph of your face on a table

#6 (close-up) My hand places a hand-tinted photograph of your face on a table

#7 (close-up) My hand places a color photograph of your face on a table

This reflexivity borders on coy cuteness, especially towards the film's end:

#235 (cu) photo of yourself, your lover and me enjoying a picnic on the grass

#236 (cu) photo of myself filming you and your lover

#237 (cu) My hand writing this text

#238 (cu) Me, filming these pages

#239 (cu) My own face

#240 (cu) My hand covers a still photo of my own face.

One can fault the forced aspect of this insistent self-reference and the tedium of a half-hour confinement within this conceptual formula (although the duration is perhaps a necessary aspect of the film's attack) as potentially undercutting the force of articulation of the film's conceptual project. Yet obsessive reiteration and coy reflexivity are common to much conceptual art. Consider Gene Barry's five-foot-square painting done in 1969, a white canvas bearing the inscription, "Note: Make a Painting of a Note as a Painting," which was part of an exhibition entirely composed of such written note/paintings announcing the "closing of the painting," apologizing that "this painting is out of style," etc.

What remains of specific interest in *Poetic Justice* is a sarcastic commentary on the necessity to read images as phrases describing events and actions (the semiotic debate discussed in chapter 2). If one is merely translating these phrases into picture representations, isn't it only a just poetic turnabout to give the viewer so conditioned the words themselves and force him or her to imagine the images so described? But perhaps the film as we view it is not just an active and creative gesture of denunciation. Perhaps what emerges is also a faint love for the relationship between words and images, a joy in that process of interchange. When seen this way the game becomes far more labyrinthine. Even the coyness becomes important to this spiraling path in which the potential visual narration and imagistic pleasure of the high angle on the table top is called into question by its reemergence as verbal description. Even "conceptual" visual art produces objects continually open to a new aesthetic and a new academy which can embrace their material intrigue. Dematerialist, conceptual artists know this dilemma, as did the Dadaists before them; but finally their response is to insist on analytic strategy that exists as much in the viewer as in the artist:

> Finally, one can't lose material conditions by simplistic "dematerialization." Objects disappear because of fundamental procedural changes in the semiotic or conceptual sign-structure of the continuum itself. The apprehension of analytic art could lie in gaining an awareness of such abstract strategies.[11]

As such *Poetic Justice* exists not as much in the space of its image or the time of its projection, but rather in the play of meanings, the investigation of image and language it suggests.

Frampton's *Nostalgia* takes up the verbal actualization of one of the recurring verbal descriptions in *Poetic Justice*, the placing of still photographs into the field of view. Each shot consists of the presentation of a different photograph which over the course of the duration of the shot is first marked by the burner coils which lie underneath, then burned until a charred mass is all that remains.

A voice-over commentary (clearly marked as a first-person narration by Frampton himself) speaks about each of the thirteen images, but this voice is always speaking about the next photo rather than the one on the screen at the moment. The asycnchronization of these voice/image units funtions to keep the audience just outside of what would otherwise to be massive self-indulgence on the filmmaker's part, the most self-perpetuated of auteurist inscriptions. This dislocation of the audience within the temporal ordering of the film places us within a memory game, forcing us to remember a commentary in order to apply it to the following image. This discrepancy creates a sense of déja-vue about each image that appears, so that we are participants in memory processes rather than just witnesses to Frampton's autobiographical revelations. The repetition of the visual stages of decimation of the photographic images implies an underlying connection between still images and memory. One is reminded of Chris Marker's film, *La Jetée*, in which the fixed still is used to evoke the oozing memories of the past. The activity of burning these images, yet recording that burning on film as another image, further complicates the graphic image's association with memory.

The film is more than a metaphor; it becomes an acting-out of a process, a machine constructed to exemplify the persistence of memory despite attempts to escape it. One can resist the film's commentary, half listen to its droning anecdotes, and yet remember enough of it to find it imposing itself on the succeeding images. This clearly shares a conceptual format with *Poetic Justice*, and even though there is a richer fascination in the image, these films represent an investigation of the signifying processes to such a concentrated extent that the evocation of force as an imaginary play is mostly circumscribed on the level of the viewing experience. This play enters primarily on the level of ideas that echo after the film (as is a goal of conceptual art).

Frampton's *Zorns Lemma* is far more permeated by gaming. Its visual games raise a series of questions. How is the acquisition of the alphabet, of verbal capacity related to the acquisition of visual recognition, perceptual fluency? How is learning in both realms historically related to an ideological placement of the subject? The title of the film, borrowed from set theory, introduces this problematic by referring to description of the shared qualities among members of a set. It also begins with "Z" and ends with "A," thus proposing a reversal of the alphabet.

The film is constructed as segments delimited on one hand by three verbal "texts," and on the other by three distinct treatments of the image:

1. Black frames, no image, are accompanied by the reading of a borrowed antique text, a rhymed alphabet poem called *The Bay State Primer*, used to teach school children the alphabet in the early 19th century. There are 24 archaic phrases, each internally rhymed, each containing a word beginning with the successive letters of the alphabet (Roman, minus the letters "J" and "U"). The phrases have explicit ideological implications such as "In Adam's fall, we sinned all" and "The Cat dothe play and after slay," teaching the child, along with the alphabet, his or her place within a moral, ethical and social system. To inscribe this reference to a past education at the opening of a film devoid at this point of images is to pose this heritage of the introduction to literacy, presenting it as a problem, without didactic commentary or documentation, only as an object to be examined.

2. This next segment of the film is introduced by the sequence of the 24 letters, each appearing on screen for one second in the same graphic presentation as the title at the beginning of the film. This establishes the continuation of the alphabet procession, as after this explicit 24 second interval, there are a series of 24 second intervals which are constructed along the order of an alphabet sign game, that is, a text, which children in play construct. In finding signs whose first letters provide them with an alphabetical progression, children mimic the form of their first book, an ABC picture book, the descendent of the

Primer read in segment one, but make it active upon their own environment. In the film, most of the words are isolated in signs found within the space of images and are associated with commerce either as part of advertisements for businesses or as place markers. Sometimes, however, the words are inserted as superimposed typed letters over the space of an image. Sometimes this ordering of the words seems arbitrary, sometimes provocative ("film, glass," "remember, shelter, think") sometimes playful or joking ("law, marchal," "thumb, under" or "hive, itch" preceded in the same series by "bee").

Then there is the further game of substituting a letter in the series with an image; each time the given letter would come up in the succession, there is instead a shot of a given subject or action that replaces it. Many of these "replacement" images are actually the fragments of a narrative action; for example, "V" is replaced by a close-up of hands peeling an orange, against a striped background, and each time we return to "V" more of the orange is peeled, then taken section by section from the frame, until by the last run of 24 seconds, now completely composed of the replacement images, the orange is gone (similar as an image of progression and disappearance to Gottheim's *Blues* discussed in the last chapter).

The order in which the letters are replaced initially has significance; the first four to be transformed are "Q, X, Y, Z," all rather odd letters, the ones that tend to stump children playing alphabet games and that have the fewest number of entries in the dictionary. Further, X, Y, Z are grouped together at the end of the series of words, so that the visual movements depicted in these images jump out as an active visual break in rhythm and perceptual space after the sign series. They are very active directional images:

Q = steam being emitted from a subway vent in New York City
X = close shot of flames in a raging fire
Z = ocean waves in reverse motion
Y = tall wheat blowing with a forceful track left further creating movement

Besides creating a variety of visual movements, these images are related as expressing the "elements" of ancient and medieval cosmologies, earth, air, fire and water, which then relates this middle section of the film to the text of the next segment.

3. The final segment of the film is a single long shot on a snowy field, with snow continuing to fall as a couple and a dog, their backs to us, walk from the foreground to disappear in the depth of the image, leaving just a white field at the film's end. The text read over this segment is an

Eleventh century cosmology entitled, *On Light or the Ingression of Forms*. The text is read by various female voices, changing at one second intervals, thus continuing the second by second pulsing of the previous segment. While the text (especially translated and read in this manner) remains fairly incomprehensible, its rhythms create distinctive patterns, and certain phrases concerning form, matter, and composition stand out.

Much has been made of the structural determinations of this film. Wanda Bershin claims that the filmmaker "absents" himself as he no longer assumes control of artistic decisions (which she gives a modernist, positive value, but which Brakhage, for example will lament as the loss of the mark of the creative individual):

> Not only does the structure lie bare, unclothed by any vestige of "content," but that structure has provided a set of conditions and allowed them simply to take their course as if programmed by a calculating machine. A 24 letter alphabet at 24 fps. provides the entire structural frame for the movie. The implication here of course is that the artist is less "responsible" than usual for his work.... Philosophically this suggests a considerably less egocentric concept of the artist than has prevailed even in the earlier decades of our century. [12]

This position ironically ignores the complex structuration of the work, addressing only a single segment, the middle section of the film. The argument assumes that decisions involving structure do not involve creative processes, and retains a critical archaism, a form/content split that would allow "content" to be evacuated, which it certainly isn't in any respect in this highly referential work.

Mark Segal has taken a similar view in comparing *Zorns Lemma* to the conceptual principles stated by sculptor Robert Morris. The artist's decisions move back one stage in the process of creativity, through what Segal calls the choice of an "a priori system":

> In film what has come under attack is the concept that a film is built up by balancing shot against shot, scene against scene, with different parts carrying different relative weights and with decisions about where to cut and what to juxtapose being made on an intuitive arbitrary basis. Hollis Frampton has rejected this method of making a film by formulating "a priori" systems which, once devised, determine the structure of the work automatically. This notion of automation, which Morris talks about, violates the conception of the "artist's hand" as the shaping factor in the art process. Of course the artist cannot stop making decisions on some level. But by removing his decisions from the actual making process, by confining them to an "a priori" status, Frampton provides his films with a solid internal logic and a structural necessity that few contemporary films share. [13]

It is my view that the structure of the film is not as detached from the process of expressivity as these authors contend, and that the double oppositions structure/intuition and predetermined/expressive are falsely aligned in the service of a proscriptive critical stance of fashionable currency. Certainly, one should consider the structure of *Zorns Lemma*, but in detail, in all its parts, conjunctions, disjunctions, references, its play of *signifiance*. In so deconstructing the film, we find that the organization serves to directly create a specific speculation on the restraints inherent in traditional language versus the challenge of visual sensitivity, the charged excess which refuses codification in the structures of language. A structural view will only hold down the process of *signifiance;* a deconstruction will suggest its play.

If this film can benefit from and withstand comparison to conceptual art it is in this inquiry into signifying and artistic processes, not merely as a reflexive pointing to its own construction, but as an extensive investigation of these processes in a social realm outside the closed set of structures which constitute this art work.

To explore this further, I must first emphasize that structuration is a process of directing interactions, not merely a frame within which the referential is enclosed and therefore contained and limited. Filmic structure is an organized space of comparison and conflict. For example, the cosmological references mentioned earlier as being inscribed in the first four replacement images of segment 2 and the medieval text of segment 3 cannot necessarily be taken to indicate that the film itself espouses a fixed cosmology, as Bershin suggests:

> Upon closer inspection it becomes clear quite soon that the film is ultimately concerned with a kind of cosmology, that is, the theory of the universe as an ordered whole, governed by a set of laws. . . . From darkness to light, and thence to life (matter) and order—the metaphysical sequence both Greek and Christian. Indeed the cosmological imagery of *Zorns Lemma* seems to summarize a cycle—that man perceives order in the universe, has catalogued it before, and will attept to do so again, in current terms for current needs. Darkness, the original mystery, the beginning of everything, turns out to be inside the mind. The overall order and general laws which are the cosmos have finally been located inside the human brain. [14]

I can see no reason for such isomorphic matching of the reference to archaic cosmologies and the film as generator of a "cosmological" metaphor, which then in Bershin's analysis is substantiated by a biographical argument (and here we must ask how the same author can argue both that the filmmaker "absents" himself and that the knowledge of his life experience should be brought to bear on the work as fundamental to its interpretation):

> It is by means of this cosmological metaphor that *Zorns Lemma* signals its most fundamental and complex concern. Having posited the *act of knowing* as the ultimate measure of what *is*, the film leads us through increasingly complex kinds of knowledge. On the simplest level, *verbal* meaning is replaced by *visual* meaning as the alphabet turns into a set of images. It is significant that Frampton began as a man of letters, as he puts it, studying languages both living and dead while fancying himself a poet. Over a period of thirteen years in New York his interest have evolved from verbal to visual modes. *Zorns Lemma* details that conversion in compacted time. [15]

Again, a metaphorical reading, a mixture of biographical and intentional fallacies constitute the critical deformation. How to restore to the film its avant-garde activity, to explore its structuring of elements as a process creating conjunctions and disjunctions and an activity of differentiation from fixed clichés?

First, consider the three "texts" which I described as taken up by each of the three segments of the film as set against each other, against an image track, against (in the first and third case) a new and critically demanding voicing of them. The complexly ordered middle section, the game of alphabets and verbal versus visual texts, is surrounded on either side by "simple" visual structures. The blank blackness of the first segment opens the film matched by a closing segment: the single shot fixed vision on a snowy field whose figurative elements (people crossing) disappear into its depth. Each is accompanied by a "borrowed" text read irreverently to expose its reference to our formative and conditioning past cultural experience, as well as to conform to the contemporary, actualized rhythms of this film text. Sound is used in a similar way in Frampton's film *Surface Tension* in which a voice-over German text, fragmented beyond comprehensibility, accompanies an extreme fast-motion tracking image through New York City. The breakdown of the spoken voice into a percussive song, a metronome counterpoint in both cases brings us back to the theories of the voice in contemporary music discussed in chapter 3 particularly in reference to *Critical Mass*. My purpose in reiterating this comparison here is to suggest that it will not help us to better understand the film to unify the thematics of its texts along with the pattern of darkness to light into a single global metaphor. The film demands that one pay attention to its disparities, its conflicts, its enigmatic gathering together of these three image/language texts. And it is certainly on this level that we must speak of compositional control, or ordering, or structuration as a gesture towards articulating a relationship between force and meaning that makes the notion of the "absent" artist presenting only a reflexive structure a most unfitting "key" concept. Let's rather speak of structuration.

A useful entry into this discussion, then is provided by Michael Foucault in his analysis of Rene Magritte's painting "Ceçi n'est pas une pipe."[16] Foucault analyzes the painting (composed of a framed canvas on an easel bearing the legend in French which translates, "This is not a pipe," underneath the image of a pipe, with another, larger representation of a pipe floating in the space above the easel) as addressing the distance between words and images. He proposes that the easel doubles as a blackboard, creating a reference to the endless labeling of primary school and textbook captioning. But through the multileveled negation, this reference becomes a didactic discourse on linguistic/semiotic interactions:

> Linked by the frame of the painting or blackboard which surrounds them both, the text and pipe underneath enter into complicity: the words' power of designation, the drawing's power

of illustration denounce the pipe up above and deny this apparition without references the right to call itself a pipe, for its unattached existence renders it mute and invisible. Linked by their reciprocal similitude, the two pipes contest the right of the written statement to call itself a pipe, since it is made of signs without resemblance to what they designate...(an unlocalizable voice) would be speaking simultaneously of the pipe of the picture, the pipe which appears up above, and of the text which it is actually in the process of writing, this anonymous being would say: "None of all this is a pipe; but a text which resembles a text; a drawing of a pipe which resembles a drawing of a pipe; a pipe (drawn as not being a drawing) which resembles a pipe (drawn in the manner of a pipe which itself would not be a drawing). Seven kinds of discourse in a single statement. But it requited no less to raze the fortress in which resemblance was a prisoner of affirmation.[17]

The "uncertain and misty region" where words and images exist in an erasure of common ground"[18] that Foucault thus analyzes is also located in the disjunction described earlier as inscribed in *Zorns Lemma*. The recited texts remain indistinct from and at odds with the images. *Zorns Lemma* is introduced by the black which lets the *Primer* stand alone, is sustained by the contrast operative in the image sequences replacing the word/alphabet sequence that produces an entirely different affectivity, and is finally culminated in the echo of segment one provided by the "*On Light*" text over the snow shot. As echo and culmination this last segment presents a gradual change across a visual field, a transformation of energy which serves not as the affirmation of representation, but rather of the potential force of the filmic image. The text which one expects to label instead becomes a rhythmic babel, whose signification (beyond the referential play mentioned earlier) is that pulse which defiantly lacks meaning.

So, as Foucault concludes about Magritte, there is a didactic discourse operative in *Zorns Lemma*, a discourse similarly engendered by the conjunctions and disjunctions of two modes of presentation. The lesson floats, it is not fixed, it is a game. A child's game of looking and listening, seeing the intrigues of 24-second shots explosively unfolding and repeating either as narrative progressions, graphic configurations and/or kinetic coloristic explorations.

The complex dynamics of *Zorns Lemma* will serve to close this chapter in which I have tried to show how diverse the inscription of visual and audial dynamic expressivity can be. Diverse and pervasive, for even those films which tend to seek a diminution of this dynamic affectivity in favor of conceptual principles end up by affirming what they apparently sought to deny. One of the ideological consequences of these avant-garde filmic explorations, then, is to confront us with the libidinal aspects of viewing and hearing films, either through emphasizing the ways in which a structuration can accentuate these processes, or by an attempt to minimize libidinal affectivity through a conceptual mode which is doomed to failing to complete this eradication.

6

Flickering Light, Pulsing Traces

All films, even narrative films emphasizing a continuity of image flow, contain an element of the phenomenon known as "flicker," due to the intermittency of frame-by-frame projection. But a light flickering at a high, constant rate appears not to be flickering at all, since as the rate of repetition increases, we attain what is known as "flicker fusion," a level at which the nerve impulses generated by the flicker becomes indistinguishable from continuous illumination.[1]

Even classical films, though, sometimes contain an abrupt fluctuation of black and white or color from frame to frame of film image, which creates a temporal pulsing and a transformation of the quality of light. In classic narrative films these instances are most likely to be motivated and naturalized by a cause, a light source within the image such as a rotating beacon, a flashing neon light or a back light from the depth of the image which is interrupted by objects passing in front of it.

In some of the films I have discussed, "flicker" or "pulsing" effects have been openly displayed without being naturalized by diegetic sources; still, in these cases, flicker is not the dominant phenomenon on which the filmic play and exploration is most centrally turning. For example, there is a pulsing of light steadily throughout *Blues* (which in fact was caused, according to Gottheim, by the fortuitous "malfunctioning" of the motor mechanism attached to drive the camera). *Critical Mass* in a different way introduced pulsing through the alternation of image and blank frames.

This chapter concerns flicker and pulsing phenomena which have been extended to define the scope of the exploration of the films in question. Many of these films are composed of abstract blocks of light and darkness or varying colors which, when projected, cause visual stimuli whose temporal duration is so brief, with the contrast so great between alternating stimuli, that the perceptual mechanisms of the viewer are thrown into such "abnormal" activities as hallucinations. These produce effects ranging from meditation calms to the sensation of being subject to the affects of hysteria. These stimuli patterns also generate such physical perceptual effects as blending of colors into white or perception of color when only black and white stimuli are "seen."

I will try to provide some physiological explanations for these occurrences and will discuss the intriguing question these films raise concerning the relation between "scientifically" based perceptual qualities utilized in artworks and the aesthetics of an economy of energy transfer that is the focus of my theoretical position. It is a difficult problem, as I indicated in chapter 4 when analyzing Barry Gerson's "studies" of modes of illumination and their transformation, since once we are in the realm of aesthetic presentation rather than the controlled and limited parameters of a scientific experiment, it becomes difficult to isolate simple phenomena and disengage the perceptual from the imaginary. The term "psychophysiological" however, already contains this paradox, for even the most recent electrochemical theories of the functioning of the brain cannot completely explain thought processes such as memory and fantasy. Psychoanalytical processes as yet remain as much within the province of art and language theory as the realm of physical science.

To consider the operations of imagery within flicker films leads to a consideration of frame-by-frame image changes. Here the question becomes even broader by entering into what has been termed "subliminal perception and cognition," the supposedly unconscious passing of signification to a subject who is apparently not consciously aware that such stimuli response is occurring. Without "proving" subliminal effects, it is certainly well within the project of force and affectivity I have been developing to speak of a cluster of associations engendered by brief images whose impact exceeds a "reading" of the image's representational statement. That excess can be understood as a tracing of either the representation or its presentation in the spectator's unconscious. The voyage of this chapter will be somewhat circular; to begin with a flicker effect within a representational film image in the work of Brakhage, then to examine the isolation of this effect in nonrepresentational work, and to return to the reintroduction of representational images within the frame of the abstract flicker film.

In my brief discussion of Brakhage in chapter 3 I argued that it was possible to avoid limiting interpretation of his works to the biographical correlations usually selected as a frame to explain his expression of a subjective vision. It seems that one of the easiest escape routes from this interpretive trap is to examine the very innovative work on the rhythm in his films. Fades in and out of light within an image are combined with the play of this pulsating light with and against other rhythms created by repetitions of distinct camera movements. Punctuation with colored leader, repetitions of patterns within the image and over the image (as in the scratched frames) also add to the play of rhythm. Although each film varies the rhythms, patterns remain recognizable, characteristic from film to film, an abstract beat which serves as an emblem (this is a Brakhage film), but which produces effects far more intriguing than a mere signature.

One can concentrate on the abstract development of this pulsing by watching the films while squinting, which reveals a complex patterning underlying the representational images. Consider *Scenes from Under Childhood,* part 1. On a representational level, the film often simulates the childlike vision of scanning discussed earlier and a polymorphic sensuality in which objects and colors figure prominently, through a series of subjective shots from a child's point of view, exploring the fragmented view of objects as diverse as other children's naked bodies and textures of the floor. Yet at moments there is an unevenness in a "cuteness" which emerges on this figurative level, a "baby picture" quality which is emphasized by the inclusion of snapshot inserts of the children seen in the film. And the filmmaker as self-conscious father intrudes marking as the narration of a personal myth what could be more interesting as a truly nonnarrative exploration of vision, fragmentation, representation and their relationship to childhood. Yet within this romantic authorial stance, the film displays a slashing of light, color, partial objects, distorted images. As Brakhage and his critics have suggested, the repeated configurations suggest that we view these flickerings as both vision and memory-return of vision, vision given the full perceptual manipulations of an active and complexly ordered psyche. Again, another limitation of the films might be the artifice of this mimesis of a process which escapes mimetic representation, whereas other avant-garde films not struggling with the approximation of a subjective interiority may be better situated to both evoke that vision and analyze it by using other structures. The squinted-eye vision of these films which I proposed earlier, perhaps points to that freer, nonmimetic exploration.

An intermediate case between Brakhage's exploration of light variation within figurative and representational modes and a purely nonfigurative exploration is offered in the film *Schwechater* by Austrian film maker Peter Kubelka. His work on flicker immediately preceeded that of American film makers. *Schwechater* was originally commissioned as a commercial advertisement by a beer company. Sitney suggests in *Visionary Film* that "Kubelka can even let the company dictate the images (the pseudo-elegant scene of models drinking beer as if it were champagne) in order to prove to them and to himself that cinema is not a matter of imagery but of frame to frame articulation."[2] I think it's too easy to claim that the images do not "matter"; in watching this film for the first time without the benefit of this historical information concerning the sponsorship, how does one react to the coded imagery being inscribed in this particular form of affectivity?

The bourgeois nature of the representation within the image (leisure and elegance) is violated by the process of reconstruction of that imagery within the flicker mode; complacent images are transformed into disturbing but fascinating ones through an excessive force applied to their ordering and functioning. If the film were shown with "Drink Schwechater" flashing on the screen at the end, would it be recuperable as advertising? Perhaps, but the perversities of capitalist recuperation cannot serve as a measure of expression. The point, rather, seems to be to understand the transformation itself, the energy transmitted through a tension of what these images would be as a continuous filmic scene and the reformulation of them as disjunct entities whose new sequencing presents a tension located between representation and the presentation of abstract repetitions, flows and flickerings of light.

Unlike Brakhage, whose light flickering works towards redefining his images within a framework as a corresponding expressive project (the formulation of vision of the psyche), Kubelka's flickering in *Schwechater* works against his images, redefining them as graphic representations whose usual codifications are now seen as historical artifacts which contribute to a new play. Consider a parallel, but inverted situation, in some contemporary artists' interest in the series in photography and lithography. The individual photo is marked by singularity and fixity of expression. In contrast, the image series may be characterized by repetition of the image altered by graphic variations (as in Warhol's various series works). It can also be a temporal series in which the change that occurs from image to image marks the passage of time. *Schwechater* turns film into an ordered series of single, graphic images, like the temporal image series of photography. However, the film reintroduces motion in the recombination of these images in rapid juxtaposition. I shall try to show how the history of bourgeois imagery is questioned, which explains the usefulness to Kubelka of these particular beer-garden images. But ultimately the entire attack by reduplication may just serve as renewal, especially if we grow accustomed to it and it emerges as a dominant and commercial mode.

There is much challenge in the systematic formulas of recombination used in the film, which includes the alternation of image frames with black frames in the following pattern ($1/1, 2/2/, 4/4/, 8/8/, 16/16. 1/1, 2/2$, etc.).[3] This black in turn alternates with a parallel block in which images are tinted red and during which a low hum and a high pitched beep sound are heard in rhythmic alternation. There are also frames of white leader. The images are also all derived from the repeated frames of just four different shots. This system constructs a film in which the image of an action is used as an indicator in a visual game of motion abstraction, bringing to mind the heritage of the plentiscope, zoetrobe and mutoscope, the various image machines which served as precursors to the cinema. By mounting a series of photos of successive stages of a movement in a viewing apparatus these machines created the illusion of an imperfect, jumpy and charming continuity of action. In *Schwechater* the linearity is renounced in favor of a play which would jump all over the spinning circle of the zoetrobe in a geometric configuration, taking pleasure in the careening reassemblage of disjointed parts as a new force.

Once the image is evacuated from the flicker film, a different functioning is highlighted. The presentation of a pure black/white alternation, a patterned stopping and releasing of projected light is the basis of Tony Conrad's *The Flicker*. The rectangular flat screen surface is the focus of the spectator's reception of this patterned presence and absence of light, although a curious secondary effect (as is true of all flicker films) is the strobing illumination of the space in front of the screen, and throughout the room of the projection. This spatial illumination increases the body awareness of the spectators both individually and as a group, although this effect varies with the room and one's placement within it.

Representation and signification through sign systems (as we know these categories at present) have been removed. What remains as the transmitter of force is an intermittent light stimulus. It will help our understanding of the functioning of this film to understand what scientists posit as the electrochemical operations in visual perception:

> It is convenient, although admittedly a gross oversimplification, to think of the pathway from retina to cortex as consisting of six types of nerve cells, of which three are in the retina, one is in the geniculate body and two are in the cortex.
>
> Nerve cells, or neurons, transmit messages in the form of brief electrochemical impulses. These travel along the outer membrane of the cell, notably along the membrane of its long principal fiber, the axon....
>
> At its terminus the fiber of a nerve cell makes contact with another nerve cell (or a muscle cell or gland cell) forming the junction called a synapse. At most synapses an impulse on reaching the end of a fiber causes the release of a small amount of a specific substance, which diffuses outward to the membrane of the cell. There the substance either excites the cell or inhibits it. In excitation the substance acts to bring the cell into a state in which it is more likely to "fire"; in inhibition the substance acts to prevent firing. For most synapses the substances that act as transmitters are unknown....
>
> It is at the synapses that the modification and analysis of nerve messages takes place.[4]

We can see from this brief summary that the entire system is based on the transfer and transformation of impulses, dependent on intermittent charges, a changing of electronic charges to chemical charges and a recharging cellular reaction metaphorically termed "firing." A refinement is offered in the postulation of an "off-receptor" operative in the system to respond to shadow:

> When such on-off cells are exposed to an edge or a step of light, they will be either excited or inhibited, depending upon whether the central part of the field of the cell lies on the bright or dark side of the edge. However, when the entire field of the "on-off" cell lies on one side of the edge—either the bright or the dim side—the cell will not fire. When such a cell lies entirely on the bright side of the edge, both its central (excitatory) region and the surrounding (inhibitory) region will be activated equally, cancelling each other. Thus, the ganglion cell will not respond to a uniform field. Instead, the strongest stimulus from an "on-center-off-surround" ganglion cell would be a bright central disc of light surrounded by a black annulus. Of course, in order for it to obtain the optimal stimulus, it is important that the disc of light just match the size of the central, excitatory region of the cell's receptive field.[5]

How does this cellular mechanism, this energy circuit, respond to the influx of light energy controlled, modeled, sculpted into a specific temporal progression as is the case with *The Flicker?*

The sensation that one has in viewing *The Flicker* (if one connects at all with its functioning, since some people resist, turn it off) is that of being brought into an increasingly intense period of affects and then back out again. This sensation can be substantiated by the patterning of clear (white) to black frames over the course of the film. Each numerical progression (there are 47 patterns in all) dominates a given section of variable length of the film: 23 clear, 1 black, then 11 clear, 1 black, $9/1, 8/1, 7/1, 6/1, 5/1, 2/1, 1/1$ and then back out again, the reversal of the pattern ending again with $23/1$. The middle section contains more deviations and irregularities ($5/1$-$4/1$-$5/1$ type changes). These figures translate as various timings of the flicker (rates of switching light on and off) from 1 per second increasing to a rate of 12 per second. The film also has a sound track of whirring noise in pulsing cycles, often sounding like the vibrating hums of heavy machinery.

Conrad has described the effects of the film as the following:

> The first notable effect is usually the whirling and shattered array of intangible and diffused color patterns, probably a retinal after-image type of effect. Vision extends into the peripheral areas and actual images may be hallucinated. Then a hypnotic state commences and the images become more intense. Fixing the eyes on one point is helpful or necessary in eliciting the fullest effects. The brain itself is directly involved in all of this; it is not coincidental that one of the principal brain-wave frequencies, the so-called alpha-rhythm, lies in the 8 to 16 cycles per second range. Hence the central nervous system itself must here be considered as a kind of sensory mechanism, though its role is not explicitly understood, to my knowledge.[6]

While there is a physiological basis to this possible series of reactions to *The Flicker,* the response varies greatly with different individuals. If one enters into the play of the film and is susceptible to either hallucinatory effects or hypnosis, the experience of *The Flicker* can reach heights of abstract orgasmic visual fantasy or can create a calmer fixation, a riveted gaze and attention.

How is this physiological functioning of an artwork related to the play of force within a secondary elaboration, to "expression" in the Lyotardian terms discussed in chapter 2? The question is complex; intuitively it is understood by many viewers who, whether pleased or displeased by *The Flicker,* question its status as "art" or "film." Ultimately the refining of the flicker effect into a distilled state which nakedly causes diverse effects only affirms "force" in the sense of a physiological response to stimuli. But when this direct stimuli is presented as an artistic project, this alteration of the perceptual apparatus at an energetic level disperses through various functions of the psyche, such as memory, hallucination, fantasy, libidinal excitement. All these functions recall various psychic effects. If the viewer is aware of alternating black and clear graphic sequences that produce the flicker, this also affects the audience's fascination and appreciation of the viewing experience. The physiological stimuli provide a psychophysiological response in which primary forces are at play differently for each viewer; adding the frame of a collective artistic experience asserts that hallucination and affectivity be recognized as part of artistic experiences. *The Flicker,* then, is a special case in the thesis of an aesthetic/libidinal economy because it posits energy's connection to fantasy.

The isolation of flicker into a strikingly bare phenomenon as it is in *The Flicker* could appear to be a unique instance of proof of that phenomenon but not a viable, expandable direction for filmic exploration. Yet it is not clear that transformations of graphic series (the alternating film frames) into projected pulses of light need be considered so limited. As yet there are few examples of flicker films so concerned with the pure affectivity of pulsating light, but in discussing *Alpha Mandala* I will try to show that there are at least some intriguing variations possible in basic light/dark patterning.

Alpha Mandala is even more an aesthetic/scientific experiment than was *The Flicker.* Its makers, Edward Small and Joseph Anderson, have described it in just such research terms in an article entitled, "What's in a Flicker Film?"[7] The goal of the experiment is to investigate the possibility of inducing a meditative state characterized by alpha-wave patterns and mandala apparitions. This state has been described by C.G. Jung, as Small and Anderson point out, "as an archetypal form which is manifest in mental images and, in turn, graphic designs and is therapeutically related to the reintegration of the psyche."[8]

The two film makers attained a high measure of success in accomplishing their stated goal by creating a film through animation cinematography which alternates black frames with a frame in which a clear (white) circle is surrounded by black. They describe the film as follows: "The spot appeared every other frame of about 200 feet of film, on every third frame of another 100 feet, and then on every other frame for the final fifty feet."[9] Later, a second version of the film was made in an attempt to counteract a feeling on the part of the audience of anxiety, according to the filmmakers. The second version "is shorter and has built-in rest periods where audiences can contemplate their afterimages for a few seconds before the flicker reappears."[10] In both cases, responses from viewers measured both in terms of drawings and electroencephalograph readings indicated evidence of the proposed effects both of simulating the mandala and the decreased heart rate associated with meditation. This serves to demystify the mental images associated with mystic apparitions in meditation by proposing a physiological basis to these phenomena.

The flicker form has also been expanded through the addition of color. The work of Paul Sharits examines both color flicker as an isolated phenomenon and as a support interacting with flashes of representational imagery. For some of Sharits's films it is useful to speak of his manipulations as a playful restructuring of the cinematic material. *Color Sound Frames,* for example, in its reshooting of the colored frames of another film so that the sprocket holes are visible as the original stock whirls past, first upward, then downward and then in superimposition of upward and downward motions, becomes a second generation artwork, existing in reference to his earlier color flicker films. So it is very easy to label this film as concerned with film material and reflexivity. But then there is the whirring, the mixture of colors, first just through juxtaposition and then through a combination of juxtaposition and superimposition, the mixture of these delightful pastel colors in motion, the delight. The film becomes a toy, a fascinating object, and again the comparison with the kinetiscope family of precinematic light and motion apparatus is apt. Even the gesture of naming the film "color, sound, frames" can be seen as an attempt to avoid a signifying construct from being laid over the bare confrontation with the experience of this apparatus; the playful interaction with this apparatus is as viable a response as is an intellectual comprehension of its reflexivity. Yet, recognition of this playful dimension has been strangely absent from critical discussions of Sharits's films, as if pleasure in perception is considered trivial beside the self-investigatory themes which have been justified by a desperate desire to distinguish in these terms alone the contemporary thrust and therefore the value of such works. We should, it seems to me, avoid a misdirected attempt at legitimation, deriving the value of films through the currency of these sorts of significations. The critic-theorist should not become obsessed with discovering and explicating the ultimate didactic purpose, with proving that there *is* meaning here. The display of the force of visual phenomena, such as a unique exploration of color in light blending and transforming over the time and space of projection need not be subservient to a lesson to be learned.

Color Sound Frames presents light and color transformations as sparkling, appealing displays whose fascination is easily understood as pleasurable, gratifying to anyone intrigued by similar color explorations in the fluid pigment flows of Morris Louis, or the subtle gradations of Jules Olitski, the juxtapositions of Ad Reinhardt. Yet the work of these painters in pigment color has achieved not only acceptance but esteem, whereas a parallel exploration of light color in film still needs external justification. Sharits, though, has other dimensions as filmmaker besides this research into the pleasurable projection of color. Within some of the same types of structures and uses of the apparatus that comprise the flicker film, Sharits will introduce discomfort, disturbance, aggressivity, and by the addition of flashing images, a whole new territory of semiotic as well as libidinal investigation of the staccato ordering of representational images within the flicker form.

The title of Sharits's *Ray Gun Virus* indicates a greater aggressivity, which is manifested in the film by a sound track comprised of "sprocket hole noise" (the sound generated by running sprocket holes past the sound head, in this case rerecorded) which sounds like a harsh machine gun blast. Also the color flickers occur in a context established by black and white flicker which is at once the absence and presence of light as no color and as a mixture of all colors. The spectrum of colors we see is placed against the context of these neutral absolutes. This contextual placement, however, takes on decidedly different rhythmic patterns over the course of the film's progression. At the beginning, we get just the black-and-white frames in rapid alternation, an aggressive flicker pattern, before any color is introduced; when color, a faint yellow, in introduced it is as a brief series of flicker intrusions on a duration of white light. Then once various hues begin to appear for longer periods of time, they are terminated first by a series of fades to black, then fades to white, which in turn gives way to flashes of color inscribed in a flicker. This intense flicker section culminates in a solid section of faint blue.

What emerges is an exploration of the patterned alteration of light, its absence, and color. From a theoretical perspective the illusions of a vibrating, shrinking and expanding screen which result from the film's play with such variables as luminosity, color perspective, and the effects of blending hues through temporal succession can be seen as creating a space of projection of pleasure and displeasure. The relaxed pleasurable rhythms which dominate at times are contrasted with frenetic flashing that assaults the thresholds of perception. The gunning sound track and a title that combines notions of science fiction, infection and attack, frame this particular flicker experience as a futuristic expression which suggests a threatening nihilistic stance. The creator is identified as a magician, not the beneficent conjurer Méliès, but an evil sorcerer who uses the cinematic apparatus to attain a sado-masochistic hold over his audience. One can "enjoy" *Ray Gun Virus,* not only through the perversity of a pleasure derived from an appreciation of a skillful offense, but because one is seduced even as one is threatened by the fleeting color glimpses, fades and flashes, the mystery of effects one has not known before. This demonic seduction is further exemplified in two of Sharits's flicker films that use flashing referential images, *N:O:T:H:I:N:G.* and *T,O,U,C,H,I,N,G.*

N:O:T:H:I:N:G. introduces some imagery into an even more aggressive, more rapid and more brightly hued flicker. The images are a clearly readable iconographic representation of objects undergoing progressive actions, yet there is a lack of contextual meaning surrounding their appearance. This lack of context amplifies the punctuated denial (of signification, of overall meaning) implicit in the film's title. A drawing of a light bulb flashes amongst the colored frames, first white, with drawn rays which are later retracted as the bulb becomes black, then melts, draining its black substance as a pool at the bottom of the image. A chair depicted in positive and negative color cinematography flashes in various stages as it falls left towards the frame edge. Two series of images—the chair is imbedded in the middle while the bulb surrounds it, light at the beginning, dark and then melted at the end. The flicker pulsations become punctuated by the image inserts, images of things, objects in a series, in an action, in a narrative sequence (bulb melts, chair falls). The title lies, there *are* things, or at least representations of things, not just flickering light. But the title is accurate, these image representations are not important as descriptions of objects. These images, whose meanings can not be stopped at the level of either proairetics (action sequences) or metaphor, still utilize both processes to generalize a sense of unsettling imbalance, of falling away, diminishing, of melting of power and material objectivity. But it is all so quick, so confined within the flicker activity, so nearly unconscious in its functioning (which is perhaps what the punctuation of the title indicates). Images of no importance reinforce the subtraction of signification within the abstraction of color flicker composition. They present another mode of articulating a tension between force and meaning. Sounds, absurd, displaced, punctuate an overall silence. A ringing phone, shattering glass, pouring liquid, a mooing cow operate as iconic auditory references that have no context, but disturb and create a further sense of imbalance.

The uneasy state evoked by *N:O:T:H:I:N:G* is an excellent example of how a gestural and associative mode can generate an affective state, a force which cannot be contained within the term "signification." *T,O,U,C,H,I,N,G* takes the expression even further, pushes it beyond the empty death of an apparent lack of clear meanings into an uncanny, highly charged state approached through the suggestive flashings of psychosexual symbolism. The symbolic castration reiterated in these images is continually intensified by a filmic structuration that works against normal narrative operations of thematization. The audience is assaulted by repetitive bursts of light, color and sound over a period of time in which the representation is fragmented.

"Destroy" echoes on the soundtrack, a one word enunciation, a poem, a sound loop whose incessant repetition blurs the recognition and even the distinct audibility of its phonemes, thus undermining the relationship between specific perceived sounds and coded significations. The clear perception of "destroy" as a coded word image is itself troubled by repetition, just as, (and this activity incidentally is another common childhood game) when one concentrates on one word, originally because of its meaning, until it looks or sounds wrong, until that very meaning is evacuated. As other critics have pointed out,[11] new words are generated by the imagined recombination of phonemes, creating such phrases as "it's off," "it's cut," "it's gory," "history," "his story," and "the straw." These phrases revolve around the signifieds of castration, emptiness, and psychoanalysis, perhaps suggesting that the auditory recombinations are conditioned by associations circumscribed by the relationship between what Lacan would call the imaginary and symbolic orders[12] (as is true in the analytical practice of free association).

The visual track of the film is composed of alternating still images and solid color flickers, organized in various distinct patterns comprising the seven sections of the film, each of which is introduced and followed by the appearance of a letter from the word "touching." Thus the title is laid over the film, its graphic form of capital letters punctuated by commas echoed in the punctuation of film segments by these capital letters. So the film is permeated with the concept of a touching which is also a separating, with a proximity which remains marked by discontinuous entities rather than continuity and unification. As a detailed analysis will show, this sense of touching as both contact and attack, a bringing together and a tearing apart, expresses itself not only in the representational images, but in their ordering as flashing fragments within the flicker activity. The psychosexual affectivity becomes a flow through and beyond representation and then back again to the uncanny presentation of a paranoid delusion, a state of fantasy projected onto the spectator. The film reflects upon its viewing as a sexual intercourse, simultaneously threat and pleasure, although this meaning is metaphorical and reductionist. The metaphor is indeed there, but becomes fascinating only as it circulates within a range of spectator response on unconscious as well as conscious levels.

In the first section of the film the solid color flickers alternate with two representational images, both close-ups of the same man, head and nude shoulders, eyes closed. In one his extended tongue is being cut by a scissors, held by a hand extending up into the frame from the bottom center, and the other depicts a woman's hand with long polished fingernails coming from the right side of the frame, arrested in the process of an attack which has just placed long bloody scratches in the man's cheek. In both of these alternating images the colors are garishly bright on the instruments involved, with the fingernails and scissors a glittering green, the scratches a glittering red. This color scheme alternates with black and white and negative versions of the same images. This alternation continues over the next two segments with changes in rhythms and solid color alternations with the third segment displaying rapid and dense patterns of alternating image flashes. This intensity is broken by the fourth segment following the letter "C" in which silence and white light flickering on the screen mark the center of the film. The man, scissors and woman's hand are absent from this segment and two other representational images are presented, a close-up of eye surgery, and a close-up of genitalia coupling. These two images in fact appear briefly in each segment, the surgical procedure given more time for recognition, the genitalia being the most quickly presented for a subliminal effect. By both inserting them in nearly hidden manifestations throughout and framing them in the middle of the film with the silence and whiteness serving to accentuate their appearance, the dual treatment gives them activity both as consciously understood elements of a discourse and as elements of the film's expression. In *T,O,U,C,H,I,N,G* as in *N:O:T:H:I:N:G* the image is rendered as diagrammatic, bringing into play clear readings on one level, in this case, the cat woman scratching, the substitute organ cut, castrated, the eye being cut or sutured, sexual intercourse. Yet the staccato presentation takes this reservoir of images and the meanings one can read in them and transforms them continually beyond these readings into new phenomena.

This becomes evident in the fifth section, following "H" in which the still images of the actions surrounding the male victim are shown in earlier stages of their development, that is, the scissors are now away from his mouth, yet open, and the tongue is extended, awaiting the impending attack, while the hand in the other series is away from the face not yet having scratched it. In the next section, both stages occur in alternation, at times creating an illusion of motion in the scratching and the thrusting of the scissors.

The final section of the film presents images of the man with his eyes open, without any of the intruding aggressive activities. This image is alternated in color, black and white, and negative with a new version of the color flicker, now comprised of a colored rectangle within another color frame. This sequence creates some curious effects, including an eerie sensation of a colored light shining behind the man, through his eyes, and through his hair when in the negative images the hair is seen as white. Then at the very end of the film, due to the color rectangle compositions which alternate with the image of the man, he appears to advance out of the screen surface towards the spectator.

The visual illusion here is difficult to register as having a basis in physiological stimuli; th spectator is likely to assume that this apparent enlarging or advance of the man at the end of the film is an entirely subjective fantasy, a response to the affects generated by the earlier images of the film. This indecidability stimulates even further the sense of the uncanny. The spectator is made to wonder about the relationship between projected representations and the tapping of internal image associations. This response may be articulated only as displeasure with the film, or as a questioning, ("why did these images bother me so much?") or as a more gratified response of amazement at the power of this artistic expression to so deeply tap the unconscious.

Theoretically the film poses the question of the relation between consciously perceived and "read" image structures, subliminal effects, and the resultant affects within the spectator's psyche. The only image in the film which is almost consistently confined to subliminal flashes is the genitalia. Does this image work as a trigger mechanism in the unconscious which then somehow merges traces it evokes or awakens with the consciously perceived images? Or, once its flashing is made obvious in section four, does this image become an articulated, consciously perceived center for the film so that we must still question the concept of a totally unconscious path of psychic affectivity (in this film, or perhaps, in general)?

This question opens up a larger inquiry located in the realm in which clear demarcations between the unconscious and the conscious are being erased. The distinctions between primary processes and secondary elaborations are retained in contemporary psychoanalytic theory, while simultaneously, the categorical and topological divisions of the psychic apparatus are being seen as conceptual models which metaphorically inscribe and suggest fixities and boundaries which are not necessarily as fixed and determined as we somehow have "needed" to pretend. The art object plays a crucial role in reminding us of the continual interaction between unconscious and conscious activity, as Ehrenzweig suggests when he proposes that the 'applied' psychoanalysis of art may backfire and modify clinical theory.[13] In a flicker film containing iconic material representing fragments of narrative sequences circulating around a thematic of castration, we can see how completely interspersed unconscious affectivity and conscious understandings can be.

This is what disqualifies Sitney's criticism of the film, in which he faults the film for being ineffective in the presentation of what he calls, the "suicidal and sexual" metaphors: "these metaphors either lack the immediacy of the color flickers or the scratches around them, or they overpower their matrix, as in T,O,U,C,H,I,N,G and instigate a psychological vector which the form cannot accommodate as satisfactorily as the trance film or the mythopoetic film.[14] My point is just the contrary, that once these images are interspersed in this discontinuous structuration, in this aggressive mode of flashing attack, we are no longer merely involved in metaphor as a secondary elaboration, in images as an articulated communication of a coded meaning. Metaphor has again given way to metamorphosis, to process, to expression, to affectivity; this film abstracts the affectivity that is present in metaphors and narratives, in what Sitney would call trance or mythopoetic films. The power of the image lies in its ability to evoke tensions, fears, fantasies not necessarily as fixed memories, but rather as vague vestiges of libidinal energies, traced in both the artist's and viewer's past.

Once we recognize this activity in the film, we can see how impossible it is to settle on an option of interpretation which pushes the film to a reflexive, material explanation or to an ideological interpretation of the projection of a paranoid fantasy. This film seen several times, on several levels of response, forces the critic-viewer to confront the indissociability of force and meaning and the constant interaction between conscious and unconscious, physical, mental and emotional activity.

I have tried in this chapter to show how flicker as a mode of expressivity can be variously inscribed, embedded in a representation, abstracted from all iconic representation, or combined with iconic presentation which, rather than "covering" the flicker effects enters into an expressive structuration as another discontinuous flashing. In each of these cases the balance between force and meaning amounts to a specific mixture of interactions, and the difference, the specificities are important. It is equally important, though, to recognize how the play with flickering light in general becomes one of the paths the avant-garde film has taken in its project of exploring the release and circulation of energy as a basis of contemporary artistic expression.

Scanning Landscapes and Collapsing Architectures:
Shattering the Grounding of the Subject/Eye

To be privileged to watch a space, a place constructed for that watching, the viewing subject is situated before the representation through its structures. This centering of the viewing subject in regard to classical representation is explored by Michel Foucault in the first chapter of *The Order of Things.*[1] Examining "Las Meninas" by Velazquez, Foucault traces a compositional mechnaism of perspective, sight lines, mirrors and architecture which come together to build a complex system of ambiguous visibility of the "imaginary" space in front of the canvas. This space is referred to (to summarize Foucault's eloquent argument) by the mirror in the depth, the turned away canvas of the painter and the gazes of the principal figures (the princess, painter and intruder) as the space in which the sovereigns are posing. Yet Foucault reminds us that in actuality the occupants of that space are the painter (at another time) and the spectator (at present). This leads him to the following conclusion, which establishes the gaze of the artist and of the spectator as the structuring absence of the representation:

> Perhaps there exists, in this painting by Velazquez, the representation, as it were of classical representation, and the definition of the space it opens up to us. And here in all its elements, with its images, the eyes to which it is offered, the faces it makes visible, the gestures that call it into being. But there in the midst of this dispersion which it is simultaneously grouping together and spreading out before us, indicated compellingly from every side, is an essential void: the necessary disappearance of that which is its foundation—of the person it resembles and the person in whose eyes it is only a resemblance. This very subject (which is the same) has been elided. And representation, freed finally from the relation that was impeding it, can offer itself as representation in its pure form.[2]

It seems here that Foucault, in speaking of representation in its "pure form," is indicating that this particular painting opens its structures of representation to our scrutiny, our analysis, our comprehension, though functioning through these same structures.

Assuming Foucault's analysis we can ask how this structuring absence of classical representation is attacked, modified or retained in the films whose avant-garde position is marked in their difference from classical and modernist tradition in that they move beyond representation into the play of figural space. In chapter 2 I approached one aspect of this question in discussing the recent theoretical recognition that the perspectival heritage of Western visual representation is inscribed in the camera mechanism as it has been developed. I proposed that one of the projects of the avant-garde has been to adjust that mechanism, to modify its functioning in such a way as to undercut the clarity and consistency of "good" perspectival registration, or to film objects arranged and lit in such a way as destroy spatial illusions of depth or to assert them ambiguously, or even contradictorily.

In this chapter I want to explore specifically the question of how the avant-garde places the subject before a spatial/temporal representation by considering a group of films which explore architectural space and landscape. To do this, it is first necessary to explore the pictorial tradition of both the architectural and landscape representation, and then to analyze the work on these traditions in a number of avant-garde films.

In discussing Schefer's and Serres's analyses of the functioning of the image in chapter 2 we saw how spatial representation and the paradigmatic opposition of architecture to landscape represents the symbolic oppositions of culture/nature and order/anarchy. Historically, it is important to note that architectural and landscape painting do not emerge in European painting as distinct genres until the fifteenth century and seventeenth century respectively. Rather, the elements of architecture and landscape serve as parts of a figuration which is centered on human figures, primarily of a religious signification.

As such, the architecture that appears consists primarily of fragments of construction which establish holy sites, churches, the city, etc. Columns, as Pierre Francastel notes, appeared in quatrocentro painting as a borrowing of a figurative object from antiquity used to create a symbolic space of representation in a manner parallel to objects taken directly from the medieval tradition, such as the pageant carts.[3] Francastel sees this as pointing to the purely conventional role of architectural figuration in this historical period.

Part of the symbolism evoked by these conventional usages is already inherent in the architectural forms to which the pictorial representations refer. Consider how Rowland Mainstone evaluates the development of the dome:

> Originally no more than the simplest form in which to construct a small shelter out of a wide range of naturally occurring materials, the roughly hemispheral dome or "beehive" shape acquired over a long period, simply as a space enclosing form, many layers of symbolic

overtones—as ancestral home, mausoleum, martyrium, temple and church. So valued for the sake of its associations than for its structural merit, it became the central germinal idea of many architectural conceptions.[4]

Mainstone's point is that architectural structures accrue social and symbolic meanings. The history of architecture manifests the development of forms and the corresponding changes in expression and signification that accompany all modifications of building construction and appearance. By understanding the expressivity of these architectures, we can then show how these meanings are either annexed by the referential system of a graphic representation, or modified or attacked by the manner in which the architectural object is graphically depicted.

The Italian Renaissance marks a particularly significant step in architectural depiction as a conquering of spatial representation through the development of perspective. As Arnold Hauser notes, art became a forum for the reification of the city as landscape, which has the ideological effect of situating the viewer, establishing him/her as subject of a new environment:

> The most important progress in advance of Giotto is made by the Sienese artist Ambrogio Lorenzetti, the creator of the naturalistic landscape and the illusionistic town-panorama. In contrast to Giotto's treatment of space, which is unified and continuous but in which depth never extends beyond that of stage scenery, he creates in his picture of Siena a view which not only for its breadth of space but also for the natural connection of the parts to a spatial whole, surpasses previous efforts of this kind. The picture of Siena is so life-like that one can still recognize which part of the city the painter used as his main theme, and imagine oneself moving about in the alleys which wind in and out alongside the palaces of the nobili and the houses of the middle class, the workshops and business houses, and on up the hills.[5]

Painting comes to remark upon the changing relationships of a society undergoing economic and political transformation by representing the images of edifices. The spectator is given a place in regard not only to the structure of the image, but (as Hauser shows by imagining transversing the architectural structures represented) the spectator's relationship to the depicted architecture is determined as well.

Certainly classical narrative films are heavily concerned with the figuration of architecture. Houses are invested with the familial, so that their staircases, fireplaces, hallways, bathrooms, closets and even their windows are elements which cry out for the unity of the family group. The Empire State Building, just months after its completion, has its intrusion on the New York skyline reified in an ultimate conflict between nature and culture as airplanes battle a giant ape in the climax of *King Kong*. National monuments become the architectural form in which spies and patriots have their final melodramatic battles in Hitchcock films. As Stephen Heath has pointed out, film narration is the constitution of a narrative space.[6] For the fiction to work, we are positioned within that space, given a structured absence within a represented architectural structure.

Once again, it becomes the avant-garde's project to disrupt this manner of figuration of architecture, and thus of viewer placement. The emergence of a contemporary architecture based on sculptural forms introduces within the architectural project of decentering, of complexly reordering space. Yet the films which I will consider as investigating a new treatment of architecture within figuration do not exalt the achievements of such contemporary building designs. Instead of a project of intertextual reification that we saw operating in the image vis-à-vis the city architecture of the fifteenth century, these films tend to choose the most banal and undistinguished artifacts of current social space and transform these spaces as part of a project to disturb and reestablish the spectator's placement, to move his/her vision into imaginary, figural space.

Ernie Gehr's *Serene Velocity* takes such banal contemporary architectural space, the institutional corridor, and through manipulation of the camera aparatus, specifically the changing focal lengths of the lens, transforms that space beyond the possibility of the spectator to place him or herself within a spatial representation. Representation is attacked, releasing a pulsing abstraction—light, color, and shapes are no longer structured to situate us in space. The film follows a rigid ordering process, based on a single camera adjustment. The camera shoots from a fixed position at the end of a long corridor characterized by its modern, institutional architecture: cinder block walls, flurorescent lights striping the ceiling, as exit sign over the far double doors, with only a water fountain, a fire extinguisher and side doors to several rooms adorning the side walls.

Gehr describes his filming operation as follows:

> I used a 16mm camera with a zoom lens. Divided the mm range of the zoom lens in half and starting from the middle I recorded changes in mm positions. Alternatively increasing and decreasing the depth of field and slowly increasing the difference between positions.... The camera was not moved at all. The zoom lens was not moved during recording either. Each frame was recorded individually as a still. Four frames at 50mm four frames at 55mm. And then for a certain duration I went back and forth... for about 60 feet. Then I went to 45-60 and did the same for about 60 feet, on to 40 65 and so on... it was a continuous progression in both directions.[7]

The resultant film begins as a very mild bouncing back and forth between two relatively similar images of the corridor. The back door barely seems displaced between the alternating images, although there is a slight jumping effect. The lights flicker, but the positions of the architecture in space remain distinctly fixed. The overall effect is the pulsating of a single fixed image. Our attention is drawn, however to a "doubling" already inscribed in the image; the corridor is divided into two halves by partition doors halfway through the depth of the image and the final door is made up of two halves which meet in the center. The image is thus symmetrically composed with deep perspectival lines. We are given the image of an architecture which extends before us as a frighteningly even, orderly tunnel. Due to the mixture of the chosen film stock and its exposure under fluorescent light, the image glows in bluish tones. The fluorescent lights spread not only reflected light on walls (as vertical stripes and on the floor as a single vertical diagonal graphically joining the vertical partition of the open doors halfway down the corridor) but also spread a general glow as loose pools surrounding the sources, the vertical bars striping the ceiling.

With just one change of adjustment (45/60) the pulsating becomes increasingly intense, and initial "imaginary" lines of abstraction occur with the appearance of diagonals to the corners. The image now sometimes appears as a series of boxes which seem to ripple in and out of each other. At 40/65 the patterns are seen to exchange places, to appear and disappear as if we were watching the flashes on and off of a neon sign or sculpture. After this, the image ceases to be easily recognizable as a corridor and there is much distortion in the frames taken with the long lens. The pulsation grows more marked and as the disparity that occurs between the alternating images becomes greater, the oscillation seems to become more rapid.

At the 20/90 position, one almost imagines that one is seeing a series of different graphic configurations (i.e. intermediary images) rather than an alternation, as the effects of superimposition have become quite pronounced. There is a partial return to the recognizability of the corridor as new objects appear on the sides of the image in the foreground, captured by the increasingly wider lens. But this foreground clarity evades us as soon as it is established and the abstract dynamics are by now overwhelming. The exposure between the images becomes markedly different so that a flicker of light (long lens) and dark (short lens) takes place. By the film's end we are absorbed in the rhythm of a pulsating, oscillating machine, an abstract light form whose dynamics cease to draw us into their perspectival representation, but rather jump out at us as an aggressive, yet mesmerizing configuration of light.

"Serene Velocity" is close to an oxymoron. As the title for a film composed of dynamic motion through a succession of stills, of representational perspectival space flattened to a surface of light pulsations and finally thrust forward towards the viewer as a captivating surrounding light, it describes the contradictions of this viewing experience. The space of representation is tranformed into an "absolute" example of Lyotard's notion of figural space, absolute abstraction which is achieved by attacking architectural references in favor of the rhythmic changes that emanate from the screen surface. Yet the "memory" of the architectural space remains even in the most nonfigurative moments of the film, so that the spectator is given the tension between the two visions as a meaning to contemplate in the film.

A similar activity involving the space of representation is operative in the four other films I will discuss as manipulating architectural constructs: Gehr's *Wait,* Michael Snow's *Wavelength* and ←————→, and Dore O.'s *Kaskara.* In these examples, architectural space is scenographic space, linked to narration and theater. Its destruction by the various filmic means of deregulating its representation also serves as an attack on standard film narrativity. The figural space opened for the spectators in this process is marked by these floating traces of a narration.

Wait is an extremely complex investigation of this dismemberment of scenographic space in a manner unlike any of the cutting patterns associated with what we have come to know as "editing" or "montage." A frame-by-frame shooting process constructs the film as a series of separate images which change abruptly. Zooms-in on the scene and jumps-back, occuring "between" frames disorient placement. Fragments of space are isolated and magnified to the point of abstraction. Lighting variations include quick exposure changes which generate flicker effects.

Yet even with all this manipulation, the brown-and-orange-toned image of the scene remains understandable in representational terms. A man and a woman are seated at a table in a rustic interior lit by a lantern light fixture, seen in long shot at the film's beginning, and reestablished by continual returns to this long shot view.

This scene of representation is also a scene of action, actions so reduced that they border on inaction, but it is not true that nothing happens, that nothing changes, that there is no proairetic code (series of actions) in this film. The narrative changes are just hidden from notice by the framing and lighting shifts (just the reverse of the classic editing system where continuity in actions hide the cuts—in *Wait,* discontinuity, disjunction in the image hide the actions).

Nevertheless, we can speak of the film beginning with the man seated on the left, facing left, the woman seated on the right, her hand on the side of her face, leaning on an elbow, and then, after an initial 15 feet of fragmented images, there is a shot in which the man turns a paper, then a bit later the woman is seen reading. At various points just such minimal actions and changes occur, such as the man looking up, the woman turning a page, the man faces right, but his chair is further left, etc. Finally at the end of the film there is a long shot of the room with the people gone, but then superimposed over this, an image of the man leaving.

Besides these minimal actions which present a proairetic sequence, there are also changes in the objects in the room. A coat which was on the fireplace is gone by the end of the film, while there is a new coat on the couch and the child's chair is moved. This shifting of objects in the room appears to disrupt a critical strategy which would assimilate the movements of the couple to minimalized actions within a narrative logic. The displaced child's chair however, is a link which serves to help explain these mysteriously shifting objects.

In the middle of the film another action occurs, another character is introduced, even more hidden than the others discussed above. Halfway through the film a child in pajamas appears behind a divider ledge in the extreme depth of the image. The child's movement is given as a frame-by-frame animation, with certain frames skipped, causing both a speed-up and a jumpiness. There is a brief second in which it is very clear that the child looks out at the adults seated in the mid-ground of the image. (That is, it is clear if one is alert, for it is possible to watch the film without even noticing the child.) The adults, however, never acknowledge his presence, continuing to be absorbed in their reading or looking in the other direction. But as the man turns his head and leans forward, he covers the child, who does not become visible again for several seconds. After this brief reappearance, the child disappears.

The inclusion of the phantom child adds many interpretive possibilities, first by suggesting a connection between the title "Wait" and the fantasy experience of the primary scene, the child viewing the sexual activity of adults. The activity here is absent, replaced by virtual inactivity; the child must wait to see, what he emerges to see remains hidden. But in this the child's position is parallel to the film's viewer; the voyeurism we are normally given on a filmic scene is fragmented into a series of image traces, flashes which in their partial and disjunctive appearance dare us to link them into a coherency which will not come, which eludes us. Thus the film becomes a fascinating placing of the spectator before a memory screen where fragments and traces beckon, taunt, but do not coalesce as memory or narrative experience. The images we see attack a notion of defined space and clear narration; their departure from the ordered logic of film editing and camerawork is what creates the opening to fantasy and the inscription of force, processes bound together in the film.

Another critique of spatial representation is found in Michael Snow's *Wavelength,* based on an intricate composition of variations and interruptions within the optical illusion of spatial transversal inherent in a zoom. The camera apparatus serves as a vehicle of depiction of an architectural space, but the studied manipulations of that apparatus will create both moments of "pure representation" in Foucault's sense, and a figural play combining sudden shifts and gradual transformations, which creates a space of fantasy, floating the subject into increasingly abstract, dislocated fascination.

To understand how this occurs, it is helpful to think of the film as taking the space of an empty loft as the stage of an event-performance, which includes among its elements four series of actions structured around the movement of human figures which are widely dispersed and isolated in the duration of the film. They are inscribed into a false "shot"; by this I mean that the film is really a faked, reconstituted shot, a zoom forward that instead of being continuous, is in fact composed of joined fragments, different rates of advance, including "jerks" forward, some contained in ellipses, fragments filmed under different lighting and filter conditions, at different times of day, on different stocks, including color negative.

The human events are conceived by Snow to be in equivalence with image events such as the changing light.[8] However, the human figure remains a privileged object within figuration, and its intrusion drastically changes the manner in which we watch the image. So if the film strives for nonhierarchical presentation, it is a striving which produces a conflict within the culturally determined codes of representation. After all, "Las Meninas" would be an entirely different painting and a shock to its epoch if its characters were absent. *Wavelength*'s radicality, its tension, is to have it both ways, moments of human figuration interspersed within a structure marked by long periods of human absence.

The human events can be summarized as follows:

1. Beginning two feet into the film, a woman leads two men carrying a bookcase from the right of the frame to the left side of the loft. They exchange dialogue ("How's that?" "That's fine.") and then exit frame right.

2. At 100 feet, two women enter, again from the right, one of them is the same woman who was with the men earlier. They move to the far end of the loft; the other woman shuts a window which had been open and the traffic noise heard for the first 100 feet of the film is reduced. The first woman turns on a radio, and as they sit drinking coffee, we hear the diegetic music of the Beatles singing "Strawberry Fields Forever." At 148 feet the second woman gets up and leaves; then at 184 feet the first woman shuts off the radio and leaves, their exits both "occurring" on the bottom right frame line. As the Beatles music is shut off, the traffic noise even through the closed windows is newly audible.

3. At 625 feet a man enters from the right, stumbles across the loft space and falls to the ground.

4. At 1107 feet a woman enters, walks to the phone and then reports to her listener that a man has mysteriously gotten into the room, and is on the floor, probably dead, and she asks for advice. She ends the conversation by saying she'll wait downstairs. Then between 1143 and 1160 ft. there are superimpositions of two images, one with the woman still there, at the phone, one with her absent.

To analyze the presentation of these events, it is important to note that the first two events are grouped together at the beginning of the film, while the third event is isolated in the middle and the final event occurs unexpectedly towards the end. Given as random occurrences, marked by a lack of development and therefore characterized as insignificant, as refusing to form a narrative signifying system, these events, in their disjunction, still maintain a minimal coherency. It is perhaps better to speak of them as the abstraction, through rarefication and ellipsis, of a narration. Being of this abstract order, the events share with the dance movements a function as gestures articulated in and articulating space and temporality. The events occurring in the interior space of the loft define that space as the space of a mise-en-scène, of profilmic arrangement, of contrived, brief references to a fiction that escapes us. The exterior space marked by the traffic and pedestrian passing contrasts with this interior human circulation. Exterior movement is documented in both its arbitrary and temporally determined (day/night distinctions) aspects.

The first two events contain indications of a concrete referentiality tied to the loft space; while being random actions, they conceivably belong inside an empty loft in the sense that architecture inscribes social functions (one moves a bookcase, just as trucks pass on the street outside). The dying man escapes this referential logic, almost as a fugitive entrance into this scene of a moment stolen from a gangster film, reconstituting the third and fourth events as departing from the referentiality of everyday life for the narrative imaginary, itself a referential cultural trace of fantasy.

Another way of looking both at the ordering of the events and the day/night opposition is to speak of the film's contradictory establishment of duration. The first two inside events exist as pockets of continuity in which diegetic sounds such as the radio emphasize a one to one correspondence between film time and "real" time of the enactment of the profilmic events. The "matching" of the zoom forward into a false continuity seems to maintain this correspondence on one level, even as it is negated by the switches from day to night to day, the flashing of different lighting, filters, the punctuation by leader. With the last event and the superimposition which gives us both presence and absence of the woman phoning, there is the negation of the weight of representation of actual space and time given the other events. This negation retrospectively places the other events into the same ephemeral and illogical order of fleeting traces which dominates the images of the film.

Offscreen space is another way in which the presence/absence conflict is inscribed. When the body falls and is left off screen by the advancing zoom of the camera, its past representation is displaced into the "imaginary space" (to use Foucault's term) existing in front of the image plane. If in "Las Meninas" the audience is equated through a structured placement to artists and sovereigns, in *Wavelength* we come to share an imaginary space with a dead man, although this formulation cheats a bit by neglecting to take into account the high angle of the shot, whereas the dead man remains off screen, below. Yet the point remains that the slow zoom effaces our placement as spectator in the same way that it comes to evacuate the dead man or to double as presence and absence the representation of the telephoning woman.

The question remains of how these human and filmic events are tied to the architectural space. On the level of pure motion occurrence the human actions define the space of the loft by creating object movement across the frame of the image and into its depth. Yet as events three and four veer away from a traditional representation they ask us to take seriously the possibility that this is an artist's loft, an atelier, a creative space of performance and transformation. As such its "empty" architecture is furnished with changes in figure movement which begin to structure a redefinition of the relationship of place to representation, when through the undermining of the concreteness of place by manipulations of the camera apparatus, a figural space (in a Lyotardian sense, of a space beyond representation) is created.

There emerges, at the end of the film, three graphic compositions hung in the space in the center of the row of windows, which come, through the increasingly closer zooming forward, to occupy the frame as a group. These tacked up images attest to the identity of the loft as atelier, as those familiar with Snow's pictorial explorations might be able to recognize them as his work, while those unfamiliar with the specifics of his artwork, can still appreciate the compositions as striking explorations of series graphics. Two are double figure compositions, the one on the left consisting of two differing sizes of the same cut out female silhouette, which Snow calls his "walking woman" motif, against a black ground; the other consists of two vertically composed photos of a woman on a street combined in a dyptich framing. The third image, that of waves of water, comes to dominate the image as a close-up superimposition filling the entire frame, a flashforward to an anterior moment when the zoom will, in its progressive (if interrupted) advance, attain this framing. It is this multiple presentation, as well as the wave photo itself which recalls Snow's photo-sculpture, "Atlantic" which is made up of a wall of thirty similar wave photos, each surrounded by the metal boxes of a large sculptural frame. This close-up photo on the still waves, the captured motion, a frozen undulation, combines to supply the film's title along with the sine wave, which, once it begins after the end of the second event, is present in increasingly high pitch on the soundtrack.

In what sense is this "false" forward projection through an architectural space, accompanied by increasingly higher cycles of pure sound, ending on the complex presentation of graphic art as framed in the film's image, a challenge to the subject's structured placement before representational images? Even if this high angle zoom where given in continuity, it would still be far from a mimetic correlate of our vision as we advance in space; a track forward at a straight-on angle is closer to imitating such spatial displacement, although even then there are obvious differences contained in the two dimensionality of the film image and the limits of its frame. The zoom which constitutes *Wavelength* teases us by exploring space along a directional path, but one whose linear succession is continually broken, interrupted, restructured, by shifts in color and lighting, by punctuating leader and flash frames, by superimposition. A zoom, a continual relocation of lenses within the camera apparatus modifies the registration so that the spatial representation which results defies relationships of proximity.

The viewer is only moved through a series of framings. The moments of holding a given lens position emphasize the artificiality of what earlier simply seemed to be a movement through space; these moments of waiting, of looking, as well as the insistent, extended duration of the mechanically achieved advance, compel one to contemplate the work of restructuring involved in the film. It reformulates this loft space rather than representing it; each gel, each color flashing rupture adds to the creation of an imaginary time and place, directing the film as a movement of imagination against representation. Linear directionality inscribed in the zoom which "transverses" the loft space, can itself be seen as a structure, an organizing axis for a series of framed event elements. The progression in time of a series of images (the film) stands in comparison to linear directionality as an organizational concept in architecture, which has been discussed by Christian Norberg-Schulz in his book, *Existence, Space,* and *Architecture,* in his discussion of the function of the path, "the direction to be followed towards a goal . . . the organizing axis for the elements by which it is organized."[9] Thus architectural structure and filmic structure in *Wavelength* exist as a figure of interchange, as the "goal" of the zoom is attained; it is both the limit of the architectural space, an element on the far wall, and yet a replacement of the image of that space with the image of another space. This other space is at once that of a photograph of the sea and the superimposition of two positions of that photograph within the "spatial" progression. This doubling of images is theoretically significant for it destroys the fixity of proximity and of closure, the marking of the limit or border, two of the qualities (along with centralization) which Norberg-Schulz suggests defines our conceptualisation of "place."[10]

Snow's ◄——————►, though in many ways similar to *Wavelength* is structured far less in a linear directionality, becoming much more concerned with a play of repetition and reversal. The organizing matrix is also camera movement in relationship to an architectural structure and to human events. The camera movement repeats itself, swinging back to recover its path, inscribing within this repeated series variations in velocity, and finally directionality, as well as variations within the mise-en-scène.

The film begins with a panning motion repeating back and forth across the exterior of a one-story building of undistinguished contemporary institutional architecture. The panning movement at one point coincides with the walking of a passerby who crosses the space in front of the bank of windows along this exterior wall of the building. Then the camera movement abandons him to return to its regular metronome swinging. A punctuation by leader separates this lone exterior scene from the interior images which follow. A long section of the film involves a similarly repetitive back and forth pivoting pan across the interior space, covering an area which at one extension is delineated by the bank of windows. The camera swings to expose the corner and perpendicular wall, including an open door and a green blackboard in the distance, revealing the expanse of the classroom space in the foreground. The attainment of the point of reversal corresponds with a clicking noise, and this accentuates the rhythm which accelerates, then slows again only to reaccelerate into an extremely rapid swishing with almost continuous clicks ending this section of the film. Continuous throughout is the sound of a motor. A mechanical apparatus pulsates its exploration of space as the sound machines measure intervals of time. The human subjectivity assigned to the camera eye looking out on a scene, moving through it in exploration, is subtracted from this insistent repetitive scanning. There are moments in this part of the film, however, which play a game with human appearances and the identification possible with these images of people, human activity; a gaming which finds an echo in the ping-pong clicking sounds that mark each limit/return. The mechanical and the human are opposed, with gaming mediating this antithesis.

Some of the human figures are used to emphasize spatial positions as their activity arbitrarily concentrates on a portion of the space. Such is the case of the couple who enter the door and embrace in front of the windows, while the pan away from them allows for their mysterious disappearance before the camera swings back to where they "should" be. Other figures are used to articulate walking motions in relationship to the pan (as does occasional traffic outside the door and windows). They are often in pace with the pan, but "flash" mysteriously in or out of the image at the beginning or end of their appearance, so that the subjectivity of the camera "following" them is undercut by their artificial introductions and departures from the image. Some of the represented human activities concern the theme of repetitious play or exchange; two figures play catch, a teacher addresses a class, a large gathering of people converses as a mock fight appears in the foreground. At the point at which the pan speeds up, a crossing figure gets fragmented as various flashed positions across six swings of the camera, creating a strobing, elliptical study of the motion, introducing the imagistic abstraction to come.

Thus the first section of the film establishes the playful inscription of the representation of daily human activity in a film machine, an apparatus adjusted to rework architectural space as in infinite series of returns established by the marked limits and reversals of a given movement. The film machine, so regulated, dominates the space, confines and defines it, imposing its mechanical order. The mechanical replaces the codes of subjective placement of narrative representational film with an entry into a different imaginary view, one of increasing abstraction, where only traces of the figures, only traces of the architectural supports and spatial references, remain. There are some of the same shifts in lighting, interior and exterior that mark arbitrary intervals in *Wavelength*. But in ⟵————➤ the new variable of velocity of camera movement is the greatest transformational factor.

Speed creates different levels of abstraction. Initially, some of the spatial indices remain, but instead of being able to sense the camera movement as a turning on a fixed point in a room, the walls appear themselves to be rocking in a see-saw motion, with a central point fixed and each "end" moving alternately forward and back as if some giant hand were shaking the entire construction. This gives way to a blurred motion when the speed increases further, creating the sensation of standing still in front of a rapidly passing train. This is supported by the "clicks" on the soundtrack now at a rapid beat, sounding like moving railway wheels. Finally, the speed is so great that at 1,050 feet into the film, the windows appear as a constant streak of light, and then at 1,240 feet, each film frame is itself a blur of color and light. It is in this abstraction, first of geometric blocks and lines of color in motion, then of blurred streaks, that the pastel qualities of the blues and pinks which have been dominant throughout the film emerge as pure configurations of hues, luminousities, and shapes. We become witness to a dissolving of representation which enables the direct confrontation with color and light expression of a different order; the space of a room, the figures of actions, and our safe positioning before this spectacle is eradicated. There is nothing to read, no objects which could give this vision a referential definition. The orgasmic moment is one of departure to a different interior, one which cannot be represented. A dissolution into energy evokes our fascination.

Other artists have been concerned with this transformation of space, this dissolving of the architecture of a room. Consider Dan Flavin's description of his own environmental light sculptures, which he calls "light situations":

> ...I knew that the actual space of a room could be disrupted and played with by careful thorough composition of the illuminating equipment. For example, if an eight-foot fluorescent lamp be pressed into a vertical corner, it can completely eliminate that definite juncture of physical structure glare and doubled shadow. A section of wall can be visually disintegrated into a separate triangle by placing a diagonal of light from edge to edge on the wall: that is side to floor for instance.[11]

Flavin's sculptures take place in a room as calculated structures aimed at undoing the defined limits of that space. Similarly, the abstraction central to ⟵————➤ is positioned in reference to the scenography which precedes it. The audience is moved through developmental stages in which repetitions, colors, and patterns present at the slowest initial velocities, within the moments of clear representation, become more abstract. These elements become traces both of anterior moments of the film and traces of nonlocated, nonspecified origin or reference, the traces which constitute figural space. This floating visual space is still linearized up until this point in ←———→ along an axis of horizontal motion and increased velocity. A shift takes place, however, to a vertical tilt at the same speed, with the level of abstraction remaining the same as in the preceeding horizontal displacement. This motion gradually slows down, until the representation of a space extending from the ceiling's fluorescent light across a window to the reflected sunlight echoing the window shape on the floor are all distinguishable. As representation is reestablished, as the speed limit is reduced to a level which allows the recognition of the referential, the human figure which appears is that of a policeman, standing outside the window, inspecting what stands in the imaginary space in front of the screen: the camera apparatus, the spectator. The titles appear, slated on a chalk board and the film appears to be over; it has traveled up a horizontal vector at increasing speed into figural space and down a vertical vector at decreasing speed. But it is not over; a coda containing as many as four superimpositions, recapitulates the images, the various moments and movements in a scrambled order, apparently arbitrary. Reversibility is established; the film ends striving for an unattainable infinity where directions and moments coexist, where the structural borders of inside and outside are abolished. Architecture, as the definition and regulation of those borders, is temporarily undone.

Superimposition in conjunction with camera movement is also used in *Kaskara,* a film by Dore O., a German avant-garde filmmaker. As she herself has put it, her film strives "to make new architectures out of old forms—like windows, a door, a man."[12] Against a sound track of extended whole-tone vowels, "ai—ee—oo" being repetitively chanted, the film opens with black-and-white still images of urban windows, many of which are broken. A superimposition of blue over these images serves as a transition to the blue tones which dominate the rest of the film, in images composed of multiple superimpositions involving a mobile, layered vision of a small house in the country, a private architectural space in a wilderness. The same man is seen at several positions within the layered image, sometimes outside and inside the house. This play of layered images is far more floating than the coda of ←———→ which, due to its position as recapitulation of earlier images, has a pre-established sense of definition covering its images, making them more "readable." In *Kaskara* the multiple vision, with its constant shifting, is the result of a process of multiple exposure performed in the camera. This creates a distinctly different treatment of light than superimpositions done in editing and laboratory printing. This shifting, layered vision is the only presentation of this space and activity we are given, while flashes of black-and-white images, including the broken window, intrude at points. We experience this blending of traces without being able to discern a meaning to this man or to this site. The traces wash by us, challenging us with their lack of temporal or spatial structure. It would not help to seek an answer in Dore O.'s biography, although the images have an origin in her experience and a meaning for her not present in their expressive presentation to us. We come away with the sense of a memory, rather than its specific meaning, a sense contained in the ephemeral glidings of structures out of placement. The signifieds are more elusive than in ◄————► which in undoing architectural structure even to the point of pure abstraction, nonetheless establishes its own clear structure as a film. *Kaskara* is perhaps more radical in its insistence on the absence of limits. It escapes structural articulation through pure repetition.

For this reason, *Kaskara* serves as a transition to the discussion of the films concerned with landscape. It shares this quality of radical reversibility with some of the more extreme examples I will discuss as revising the coded inscriptions of landscape representation and expanding the exploration that painting began of light and abstraction within the landscape genre.

The landscape tradition in painting can be traced as an independent genre (that is, not just background space or the type of city views that Hauser discussed in the Siena painting in the citation at the beginning of this chapter), to the seventeenth century. It is a genre of painting which from its inception contained significant implications for the evolution of pictorial abstraction, a point made by Ehrenzweig and explained also by John Berger in his book *Ways of Seeing*:

> The sky has no surface and is intangible; the sky cannot be turned into a thing or given a quantity. And landscape painting begins with the problem of painting the sky and distance.
>   The first pure landscapes—painted in Holland in the seventeenth century—answered no direct social need (as a result Ruysdael starved and Hobbema had to give up). Landscape painting was, from its inception, a relatively independent activity. Its painters naturally inherited and so to a large extent were forced to continue the methods and norms of the tradition. But each time the tradition of oil painting was significantly modified, the first initiative came from landscape painting. From the seventeenth century onwards the exceptional innovators in terms of vision and therefore technique were Ruysdael, Rembrandt (the use of light in his later work derived from his landscape studies), Constable (in his sketches), Turner, and at the end of the period, Monet and the Impressionists. Furthermore, their innovations led progressively away from the substantial and tangible towards the indeterminate and intangible.[13]

Landscape painting uncovers painting's possibilities not to merely represent objects but to explore the relationship between light and vision, between color and light taking into account the transformational qualities of pigment and canvas. Avant-garde films whose figuration involves landscapes display parallel concerns.

Cinematography transforms spatial atmosphere similarly to the projects of Constable and Turner. Films that actively explore landscape are more directly reminiscent of Monet's studies of the haystacks and the Rouen cathedral, where variables of time of day are marked by the shifting color systems. The radicality of these filmic investigations, (what distinguishes their functioning from being a mere repetition of the impressionist project) is twofold: first, these films introduce the temporality of cinema into an investigation of what was always a temporal as well as a spatial phenomenon; and secondly, the landscape/atmosphere films do not involve a mimetic gesture of pigment application, but rather concern the varying degrees to which adjustments of the camera mechanism produce images in which mimesis is a variable. The filmmaker thus uses his or her knowledge of film stock and the camera apparatus as a reservoir of potential variations, which in the exposure of film images entails a process of selection. The formation of the image can be understood as a mechanical and photochemical process which the artist composes to bring forth relations of color, light, atmosphere, and degrees of referentiality and abstraction. As such, a technology, that of the camera apparatus, confronts nature, transforming it. The manner in which this confrontation of artist, machine and nature takes place is inscribed in the image traces which comprise the film. The culture/nature paradigm is therefore inherent in films studying landscape.

This inherent paradigmatic opposition is evident in the discussion of Gottheim's *Fog Line* in chapter 4, where I analyzed how the changing atmosphere enveloping a landscape is registered in the film as gradual transformations of the attributes of the projected image. Here the nature/technology interaction is accentuated by fixing the camera in space and allowing the temporal succession of the cinematic image to play with the inverted dynamics of the lifting fog and increasing iconic recognition.

I also showed in chapter 4 how the treatment of landscape in *Barn Rushes* structures repeated takes, each presenting slightly varied light and spatial relationships. Another of Gottheim's landscape films, *Horizons,* combines and complicates the type of formal abstractions operating in the two shorter films discussed earlier.

At first it might appear that *Horizons* does not display the same degree of abstraction, since the images depict a landscape changing according to a seasonal cycle and is firmly based in the representation of a referential world. We are shown images of the cultivated terrains of agriculture, a rural life which includes human activity undergoing the physical and social changes associated with a temperate climate. At points these images come alarmingly close to calendar photographs and border on the pure romanticism of glorifying nature's return to "life" (a summer, fall, winter, spring succession that has lent its power of naturalizing faith to many narrative films, but most notably to the greeting card punctuated segments of *Meet Me in St. Louis*).[14]

So we must ask if and how the film escapes a visual coding that has become a cliché. These landscape images would present the obvious if they were to be taken as only the representation of the qualities of the seasons, as a result of a reduction of the image to a singular verbal code, a reading according to representation alone. The film resists such a reading by its concentration within each shot and segment on the internal examination of the composite of visual elements, and their repetition and variation in a formal structure. It is not that the presence of snow denotes winter that is of importance, nor is winter being illustrated for the nostalgic; rather winter provides a series of images exploring black, brown, grey and white and a stillness filling a space. This same space in other segments is filled with movement and different colors. These seasonal changes carry an uncanny fascination which becomes vital in the intersegmental relationships drawn by the film. Thus the film's structuration, a systematically patterned montage of images, intensifies the concentration on the abstract differences and similarities in composition. This structure is described by Gottheim as follows:

> The first section, Summer, is so to speak, a little lexicon of shot relationships, of pairs of shots, brought together according to various associational principles; doublets that can be thought of as "rhymes." This principle of pairing is carried forward in the rest of the film. In the second section, Fall, the middle two shots of each four shot unit constitute a contiguous doublet of the sort that is now familiar to the viewer, but the rhyme of the outer two shots must leap over the middle pair (in the ABBA pattern). In blue winter we leave contiguous pairings behind forever; now all elements of the pairs must connect with their mates in an interweaving dance (ABAB) and in Spring, the pairs have produced offspring, there are now triplets cavorting not just within a unit (which in all sections, one second of colored leader tries to fence in) but fleeing from unit to unit like flying gnats in terza rima. (In the terza rima of the *Divine Comedy* the central element flanked by the chiming outer pair points forward to the next chime, ABA BCB CDC ..., here that lone central shot casts a wistful backward glance at the chime that preceded it, BAB CBC DCD ...)[15]

Gottheim goes on to discuss how this pattern affects the viewer's vision, "bringing into prominence a certain movement, color, shape, event which might otherwise be subordinate." Yet the degree to which a pattern is recognized or even exerts an influence over what elements are perceived is a subjective process, changing with the kind of attention the viewer brings to the film. This provides a meaning for the title beyond its more obvious reference to the multiple, repeated views of hills creating high, arching horizon lines throughout the film. This meaning, Gottheim tells us, is a reference to Husserl's *Cartesian Meditations,* where he speaks of the "horizon" of every subjective process as the degree to which possible patterns are perceived and experienced.[16]

So *Horizons* places the representations of landscapes in the context of image perception and montage to emphasize the "indeterminate and intangible" (as Berger expressed visual abstraction). Since these landscapes provide a variety of colors, shapes, textures and movements that can be framed and reframed, they provide excellent material for this creative gesture. Knowing that the filmmaker lives in this space, worked with the filming of it for two years, is another way of seeing the artist drawing on the material of nature and daily life. The viewer is not placed within the sphere of the representation of that external reality, so much as he is enveloped in the expressive activity of the images in their filmic ordering.

It is with this sense of the "enveloping" art work that we return to the theories of Erhrenzweig and Lyotard, to recall that these theories are often directly articulated using the example of Cézanne's work in transforming the pictorial space of both the still life and landscape traditions. While Ehrenzweig only speaks of the still lifes, his analyses of Cézanne's "form distortions" as evoking an overlay of "peripheral distortions," which normally undergo "repression from the final memory image" of conscious undistorted perception,"[17] holds for the landscapes as well. Cézanne becomes a pivotal figure in Ehrenzweig's analysis since he "worked in the twilight between traditional and modern art, between realism and manifest thing destruction in abstract art."[18] The films discussed in this chapter remain in a mode of abstracted representation as well, and even though Cézanne's distortions as painterly operations are different from those of the films, we shall see how the theoretical approach of Erhrenzweig has a parallel applicability to aspects of filmic abstraction and distortion in the landscape films.

Lyotard addresses Cézanne's landscapes directly, and while he places them in a similar comparison to the nonobjective concerns of Klee, Delauney and Kandinsky, his analysis of their functioning is less concerned with unconscious perception than it is with imaginary space. The discussion is in the context of his argument critiquing other methods of "applying" psychoanalysis to art, which remain bound to the reading of symbolic figuration within representation. Lyotard wants to show that the unconscious is active in the act of painting and viewing, and is channeled, directed, fixed, rendered inactive by representation.

In order to present his argument, Lyotard contrasts two periods in Cézanne's landscape painting, a period (1882-1887) where "a connected system prevails over mobility," and "space crumbles and blocks the circulation of chromatic fluctuations" and a later period where these constructivist restraints are undone. Lyotard claims that "the compulsion for ascendancy is effaced, the construction becomes almost floating, space is disconnected, the compartimentalizing drawing disappears, the canvas itself becomes a libidinal object, pure color, pure femininity."[19]

Thus representation and the semiotics which would analyze signifying processes of scenographic space are seen by Lyotard as parts of the same constraints over the development of painting as a libidinal surface which has no "principle of organization or action outside itself (in a model to imitate, in a system to respect)."[20] In reference to the last paintings of Cézanne, the late views of Mont St. Victoire, Lyotard sees another example of figural space where landscape and space are thought of quite differently as infinitely unfolding extensions of the imaginary. This space is not a depth, but an impenetrable surface; the reduction of representational depth in favor of surface texture has been one of the formal tendencies of post-Cézannian art, well elaborated in the criticism of Herbert Read and Clement Greenberg among others. Yet it is only within the psychoanalytic theories of Erhrenzweig and Lyotard that his formal tendency is explored as affecting the activity of the unconscious, on one hand through the manner in which it revives unconscious perception and on the other, its release of the imaginary from the constraints of the symbolic.

Still, it seems too convenient and hasty to brush aside those aspects of Cézanne's late paintings which would intrigue the practitioner of a semiotic approach that Lyotard denigrates. Lyotard fails to consider the consequences of the Mont St. Victoire paintings forming a series, all titled in reference to a unique white mountain just outside the painter's home in Aix-en-Province, and ranging in degrees and types of abstraction. Looking over the series, one is struck by the relative depth versus impenetrability, by the changes in the use of paint, color and blank canvas, and the consequence of these changes for the processes of signification. Even the canvases, which in historical retrospect appear startingly like Klee's pure color divisions of surface space, exist in relationship to the most clearly delineated views of stucco houses amidst foliage, dominated by the ascending angles of the mountain. This is not to contradict Lyotard's main and important argument; but rather to reiterate the cautionary statements made in chapter 2 that a semiotic analysis can and should exist side by side, in alternation with that of an aesthetic economy.

This is particularly important in discussing films which develop their imagery out of the space of landscapes. In order to adapt the theoretical formulations of Erhenzweig and Lyotard to cinematic expression, I will examine two films, Werner Nekes's *Makimono* and Michael Snow's *La Région Centrale.*

The title "Makimono" suggests a different approach to landscape than that found in the Western tradition; the film is named after the diagonally organized Japanese landscape scrolls, indicating a parallel to what the occidental observer has termed "bent perspectives" in Oriental art. The titles continue this reference to the scroll as red letters unroll to the left on white background. The basic landscape reframed and rescanned by the film consists for the most part of a lake, mountain and sky, dominated by blue-green tones, though there is another "scene" which includes a field and a house.

The film is developed as three sections delineated by the Anthony Moore sound track. This three-part composition produced on a sound ring modulator and mixer parallels the increasing complexity of the image activity from section to section. Nekes has described this composition as follows:

> The first section is a straight forward pair of sustained pulses remaining in a fairly fixed relationship to each other. The second is a single oscillating wave recorded twice and with the vari-pitch control the waves are made to interfere, phase, echo, rhythm, etc. In the first part of this piece the lowest string of a bass is bowed, harmonics emerge. The third consists of rhythmic pulses and tuned tones using techniques from both the first and second pieces, accompanied by two toy pianos.[21]

Correspondingly, the images of the first part are more defined in their singularity or more simple superimposition patterns, due in part to their fixity, than are those of the later sections. At first the camera is fixed on various long shot positions along the axis of a horizontal pan, although the camera is never moved while shooting. The field of view along these horizontally displaced images begins with a pattern in which shot B represents a displacement to an area which partially overlaps along the left of its frame with the field of view found to the right of the preceding image A. The images are each held as a layer of superimposed imagery (all shot as such in the camera) dissolves in and out, so that it becomes impossible to speak of "shots" per se. Later in the section, this displacement contains no overlap—each image is precisely contiguous space. The supers build up to a density of five images and then this first section terminates with images of people walking across a field which is empty, except for a house. The people change positions or are absented from the images according to a pattern that defies temporality. Like ◄————► this changing figuration also disturbs our notion of the represented space as constituting a place, a disturbance which is furthered by extreme fluctuations of light.

The second section of the film returns to various images of the lake and mountain area, with the image angles now varied along a vertical axis. The various superimposed layers are shot with varying focal lengths, a procedure which increases the spatial ambiguities. Horizontal panning motions are introduced: at first the speed of the pan is consistent in all layers of the superimposition, then the speeds vary between layers. Later the various superimposed pans not only vary in speed, focal length and level on the vertical axis, they also vary in direction, so that two levels of imagery will be panning to the left for example, while another layer pans to the right. This section culminates in two circular panning layers being superimposed with one in which a wave motion (diagonals up and down within a circular pan) is introduced.

In the third section, single-frame shooting is added, skipping frame by frame to various positions along the horizontal and vertical axis. Nekes speaks of his work as involving the disjunction of space, frame-by-frame which he calls the "filming of time or place difference between separate individual frames"; the mystery of the absences is evoked by his phrase, "whatever happened between the pictures?"[22] Again, the variables of changed focal lengths, angles and light exposure are all involved as frames are taken from all directions in an imaginary sphere in which the camera is centrally placed. The film ends with the super of two circling pans in opposing directions in which all variables in the image registration are in fluctuation.

The simultaneity of different views and the scanning techniques found in *Makimono* can be seen as the filmic evocation of the processes Erhrenzweig describes, but in film there is a great historical and technical difference that must be taken into account when one speaks of these processes as applied to the generation of new images. *Makimono* presents this scanning and layering systematically and emphatically through the careful design of multiple possibilities open to the camera which are not available to human perception. The delicately colored layers of images become the combined turbulent traces of perceptual variations; memory as well as unconscious perception is being evoked. Film changes the temporality of the experience, as simultaneity, duration and movement here are of a new order.

In its unfolding this filmic scroll exists in time and in a series of variations that Erhrenzweig does not address when speaking of the tableau as his model in his discussion of the extended stare before the fixed image. However, Erhrenzweig does discuss "time-free" music in relationship to Bach's reversal of the polyphonic structure of a fugue in his "Kunst der Fuge." He goes on to discuss Schönberg's more radical reversals, which along with Schönberg's use of atonality, eradicate the balance still predominant in Bach. He suggests a manner of understanding unconscious perception as an accumulation over a period of time of effects lost to conscious perception bound as it is to a temporal progression and units of articulation.[23]

Makimono gains its impact by continually denying the "shot" as a unit of filmic articulation, either by superimposing images or by frame-by-frame changes. The film builds a tension between the fixed camera position at the center of the world it explores and the extreme mobility of image that destroys the shot as fixed site of a single image. This tension undercuts any secure place for the viewer within a scene of representation. If we make out, at times, a lake or mountain before us, the momentary certitude of that representation soon floats away in the onrushing imagery that refuses to remain framed and fixed long enough for us to establish ourselves before it. A film like *Makimono* creates a new kind of imaginary landscape, one that turns, not as Cézanne's framed tableaux turned, but in a manner specific to the cinematic apparatus.

Lyotard has come to realize this difference, this specificity, when, in his essay, "The Unconscious as Mise-en-scène,"[24] he turns to *La Région Centrale* as his example of an aesthetic economy that attacks a Freudian aesthetic of the mise-en-scène of the unconscious and desire (which Lyotard finds grounded in the model of the official late nineteenth-century Viennese theater and opera). Lyotard points to the film's destruction of the frame, its destruction of any identifiable geometric space of representation, its atemporality and/or multitemporality as factors which make this film apparatus at least somewhat analogous to his notion of the unconscious. His analogy claims that the unconscious cannot be staged or interpreted, but exists as a device which can be described, just as Snow's film becomes such a device (but he modifies the analogy by distinguishing the difference in talking about an apparatus operating on drive material and one operating on visual material).

I would like to open the enclosure Lyotard has built for the film within this analogy by examining how *La Région Centrale* performs as a film on the visual material of landscape. In the formation of his critical metaphor, Lyotard accounts for both our knowledge of the film's generation by a specially constructed machine programmed for the movements through which it carries the camera, as well as for the traces of landscape representation that exist in the projected film. But this accounting is to serve the metaphor, not, as Lyotard admits, to examine "the work done on each of the parameters of traditional cinematographic representation" nor to analyze the visual and auditory experience which affects the viewer. It is my interpretation of these aspects of the film which leads me to see the film as less extreme in its radicality than Lyotard suggests, for besides an apparatus operating on visual material, there is that visual material, in both its force and signification, projected for the viewer.

The rotation of the camera through a landscape of barren rocky terrain and sky by a specially constructed levered machine creates a film comprised of traces of this trajectory. Turning in circles, the camera is always in motion, but speed and direction remain variables establishing patterns in each of the film's seventeen segments. As Snow has said, "the camera moves around an invisible point completely in 360 degrees not only horizontally, but in every plane of a sphere. Not only does it move in predirected orbits and spirals, but it itself, also turns, rolls, and spins."[25] The segments of varying lengths and types of movements and imagery are delineated by white X's against a background which fills the screen as a jarring graphic stasis before the next whirling excursion.

Knowledge of the technology involved, the special apparatus constructed to attain this unique movement provides one way of approaching the film theoretically. The shadow of the mechanism appears several times in the image, but our knowledge of it is also dependent on external information which Snow has provided,[26] and which is often given in program notes accompanying the screening. This includes knowing that Snow "only looked in the camera once" so that the direction of the film was made by a system of remote control. The sound patterns correspond to the image changes throughout, so that the signalling patterns become an indicator for the audience although with occasional deviations. Thus machinery, always a component of cinematic creativity and expression, is here placed in a new, insistent contact with the viewer. The images seem to appear without human presence or intervention. But we also know that Snow designed the film by dreaming up this machine and commissioning its construction. The images produced, while uniquely available through the mechanical apparatus, evoke similar visual experiences which partially share these spinning, reversed visions. The film systematically explores aspects of vision attained by the child turning his/her body around in a mock pirouette until he/she falls dizzy to the ground, or hanging upside down from a swing or bar, or moving his/her head along a horizon. The pleasure of mobility of the eyes gained by a childlike freedom of exploration of space with the body is recalled in *La Région Centrale* by a compendium of camera movements and effects of changing velocities.

The film also asserts the frame and the cinematic image as formally abstracting the landscape, turning the horizon line into an abstract striping, circling as a diagonal line across the edges of the frame or becoming a strong vertical demarcation, as rectangular areas of brown and blue within the rectangular frame. Another abstraction is that which transforms earth textures delineated in clear focus and bright light into blurs of color. At other points the earth/sky alternating cycles are so rapid that the blue/brown alternation flashes across the screen. The historians of art who trace the lineage of pictorial abstraction to landscape have presented another theoretical entrance into the film, for it becomes a continually changing reference to the various graphic configurations explored by recent nonobjective, large-canvas painters. The glowing color, the light and the presence of movement and change are, however, unique to film.

This endless turning and these various abstractions tend to establish a sense of reversibility of the film, of its occupying a duration, but one so infused with a pattern of repetition and variation that the order of the seventeen segments could be scrambled. Yet there is a progression through time in the representation of a day which turns into night and is followed by a dawn, becoming day once more. The film does not relinquish its hold on the recognizable, the landscape, the day/night cycle, even as it carries its work of subversion and abstraction of representation to an extreme.

So finally, *La Région Centrale* and *Makimono,* as well as the other films discussed in this chapter, exist in relation to a history of representation of architecture and landscape, as well as to the placement of the subject in the act of viewing either those representations or the scene which surrounds the body in space. They play with that sense of space as it fixes itself as representation or drifts away. Their expressive force is within this tension, a movement back and forth or circling throughout the interlacing of the imaginary and the symbolic.

The different kinds of films examined in this study explore the relationship between force and signification in various ways. I have suggested, though, that the affects of force are sharpened and made apparent to the viewer of the films due to the destruction of standard types of narrative development and the established codes of discourse in filmic (pictorial and auditory) expression. I have tried to show how these films demand a viewing which takes in a speculation on perception, illusion, conjunctive and disjunctive relations of signifiers, the history of representation and its spatial constraints in visual art, and the processes of the unconscious in the viewing subject. But I have emphasized that the questions are posed even as the mechanisms they interrogate are in effect. The films are not often metacritical discourses (and can only be partially so given the type of processes they would examine). They are objects whose presentation is oblique, whose functioning remains to be discovered. This is not to suggest that one cannot discover lessons about representation, film viewing, etc., in them, but the current critical esteem for metacritical reflexive operations in art seems to miss the point that the artistic apparatus/object in this case retains a direct affectivity, a libidinal play which it can not afford to dismantle. For if its reflection is on fascination, it cannot fail to fascinate, which means to disguise as well as disclose.

How, then, does it become relevant to suggest that the films present new visual and auditory ideologies? Only in the most restrained, cautious manner. If the history of artistic representation has been tied to analogy and reference in the production of meaning, these mechanisms are used differently in these films. The films become a space and time which move away from, return, and then depart once more from these operations of analogy and reference basic to the nineteenth-century pictorial heritage of the camera and the fidelity to voice and sound sought in sound recording historically. They can be seen as questioning the dominance of that visual and auditory tradition. In their departures these films ask us to see an expressivity in abstraction, to understand our looking and hearing as an investment of the psyche, as an activity whose range delves into the unconscious, as well as various types of conscious reactions simultaneously. Meaning is not absent—it is largely plural. But certain meanings are not present.

The absent meanings are those which articulate clear social critiques and means of social change. What do these films have to offer a society faced with crushing social problems? These films are not instructive argumentations for political thought and action in the manner that the discourse of documentary or fictional narrative can be. But this statement merely tells us that these films can never replace other forms of filmmaking in which storytelling and informing are the goals.

Avant-garde filmmaking is another practice, another exploration. There is a film which examines the ideological implications of comparing these three distinct filmmaking practices (which nonetheless always overlap): Nagisa Oshima's *The Battle of Tokyo or the Story of a Young Man Who Left his Will on Film.* In this film of narrative fiction the characters are struggling with a debate pitting the political commitment to filming documentaries of demonstrations against the government versus the obsessive need to create an avant-garde film. The images of the avant-garde film are criticized by the Leftists for not being readable as political discourse and they therefore find them to lack meaning and to be worthless trash. Oshima's fiction suggests, however, the psychoanalytical basis for the avant-garde film's attraction for its filmmaker and the one appreciative viewer it gains among the members of the political collective. The mystery of the imaginary, of the subject's past, of desire, of sexuality, of exchange, of violence is not represented in the avant-garde film's images, but is obliquely presented in the refusal of these images to provide clear references and meanings. This mystery becomes the fascination for the subject. At one point in the film, the avant-garde film is projected onto the body of its viewer, a visual metaphor within the fiction for the avant-garde film's functioning. The heroine masturbates as the images become a tattoo of changing traces and flickerings. She recalls in the space of this projection the trauma of her recent past, the departure of her lover on the day of his death. This is the history she traces over the film, just as I traced a story over *Lemon* and the other films discussed in this book: a story of desire, pleasure, pain, of the network of the psyche connecting unconscious and conscious activity.

My point is not (nor is Oshima's) that one can retreat into the realm of intrasubjectivity of libidinal economies and ignore the exigencies of political activity. I am, however, deeply concerned with experiencing and thus learning about the psyche, and value the affectivity as much as the knowledge. The avant-garde film becomes an important stimulus to such concerns, and it has been my position that this object of interaction must be recognized theoretically as an apparatus capable of bringing to our attention the force contained in filmic expression.

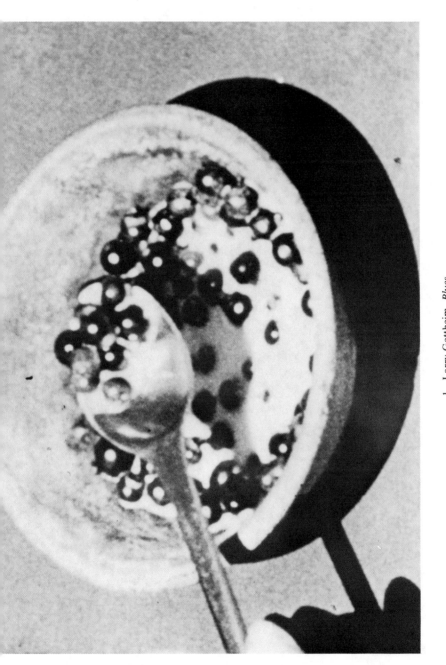

1. Larry Gottheim, *Blues*

2. Larry Gottheim, *Fog Line*

3. Larry Gottheim, *Barn Rushes*

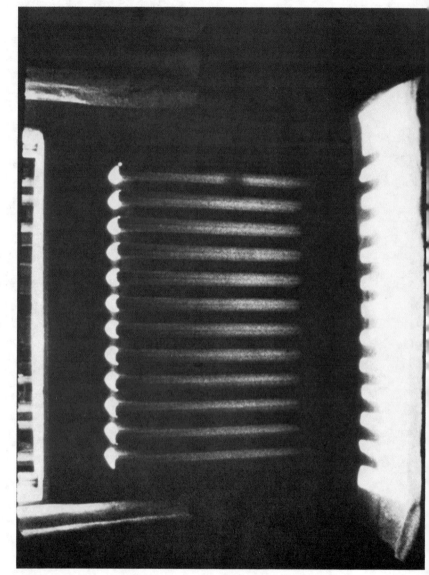

4. Barry Gerson, *Luminous Zone*

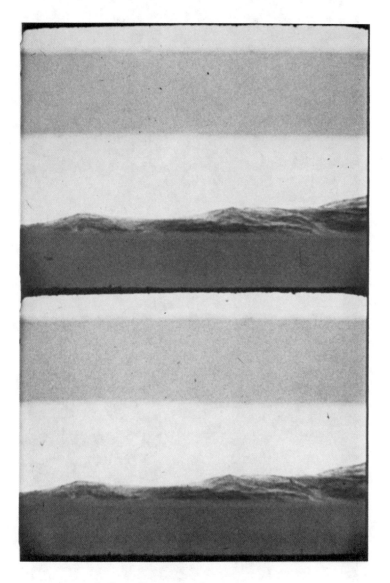

5. Barry Gerson, *Translucent Appearances*

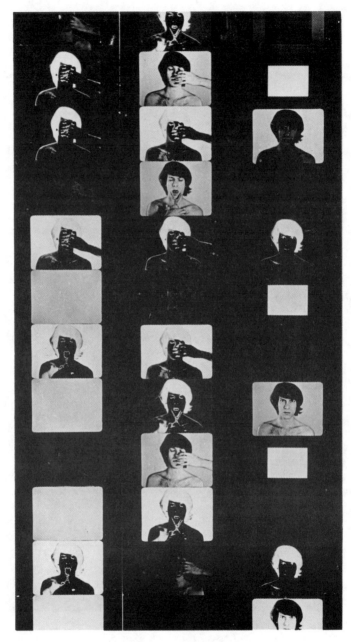

6. Paul Sharits, frames from *T,O,U,C,H,I,N,G*
(Courtesy of Whitney Museum of American Art)

7. Michael Snow, *Wavelength*
Photography: National Gallery of
Canada/Galerie nationale du Canada.

8. Michael Snow, ◄────►
Photography: National Gallery of
Canada/Galerie nationale du Canada.

9. Michael Snow, camera apparatus for *La Region Centrale*

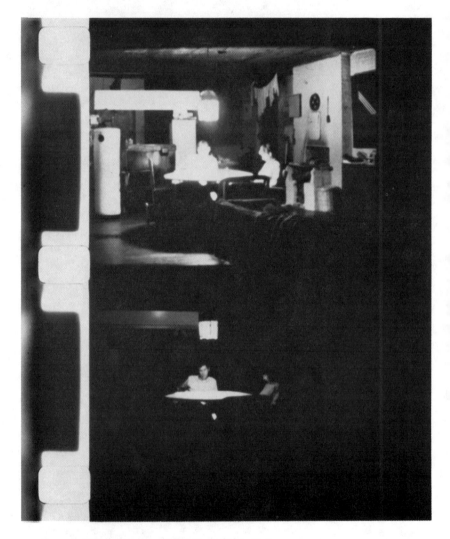

10. Ernie Gehr, *Wait*

11. Ernie Gehr, *Wait*

12. Ernie Gehr, *Serene Velocity*

13. Hollis Frampton, *Winter Solstice (Solariumagelani)*
© Hollis Frampton Estate

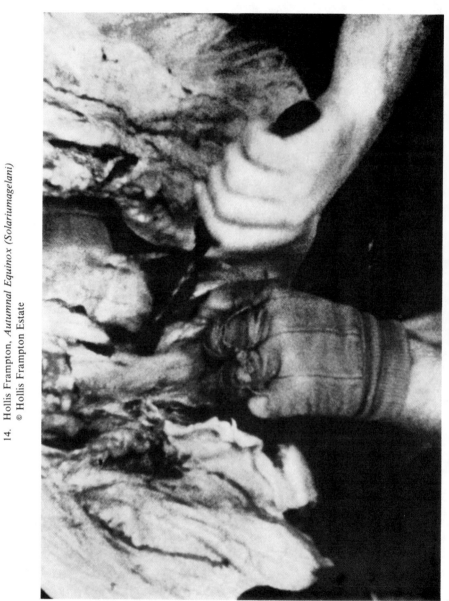

14. Hollis Frampton, *Autumnal Equinox (Solariumagelani)*
© Hollis Frampton Estate

15. Hollis Frampton, *Zorns Lemma*
© Hollis Frampton Estate

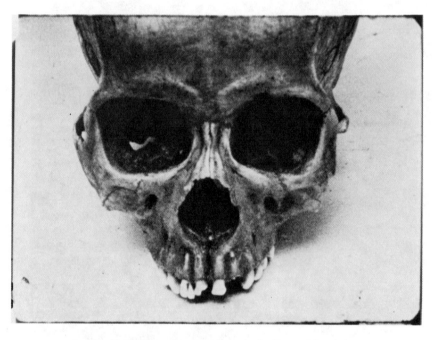

16. Hollis Frampton, *Magellan: At the Gates of Death*
     © Hollis Frampton Estate

17. Larry Gottheim, *Horizons*

18. Larry Gottheim, *Mouches Volantes*

Notes

Chapter 1

1. Jacques Derrida, *Of Grammatology*, trans. Gayatri Chakravorty Spivak (Baltimore: Johns Hopkins, 1976), p. 70.

2. Julia Kristeva, *Semioteke, Recherches pour une sémanalyse* (Paris: Editions du Seuil, 1969), and *La Révolution du langage poétique* (Paris: Editions du Seuil, 1974).

3. Christian Metz, *Language and Cinema*, (The Hague: Mouton, 1974) pp. 121-28.

4. Roland Barthes, *S/Z*, trans. Richard Howard (New York: Hill and Wang, 1974), pp. 3-16.

5. Noel Burch, *Theory of Film Practice*, trans. Helen R. Lane (New York: Prager, 1973), and Christian Metz, "Syntagmatic Analysis of the Image Track," *Film Language*, pp. 149-84.

6. Christian Metz, *Essais sur le cinéma*, (Paris: Klinksieck, 1973), II.

7. Jean-Pierre Oudart, "La Suture," *Cahiers du Cinéma*, no. 211 (avril 1969), pp. 36-39.

8. For further discussion of this see my unpublished master's thesis, "The Textual System of *Au Hasard Balthazar*," (University of Wisconsin, 1975).

9. Metz, *Language and Cinema*, pp. 101-103.

Chapter 2

1. Roland Barthes, "Rhétorique de l'image," *Communications*, no. 4 (1964).

2. Ibid., p. 5.

3. Ibid., p. 7.

4. Umberto Eco, *La Structure Absente* (Paris: Mecure de France, 1972), p. 178.

5. Ibid., p. 217.

6. Christian Metz, *Essais Sur le Cinéma*, (Paris: Klinksieck, 1973), II.

7. Jean-Louis Baudry, "Effets idéologiques produit par l'appareil de base, *Cinéthique*, no. 7/8 (1970), pp. 1-8, trans. Alan Williams, "Ideological Effects of the Basic Cinematographic Apparatus," *Film Quarterly*, 27, no. 2 (Winter 1974-75), pp. 39-47.

8. Ibid., p. 41.

9. Ibid.

10. Ibid., p. 43.

11. Roland Barthes, "Le Troisième Sens," *Cahiers du Cinéma,* no. 222 (juillet 1970), pp. 12-19, trans. as "The Third Meaning," *Artforum,* 11, no. 5 (January 1973).

12. Jean-Louis Schefer, *Scénographie d'un tableau* (Paris: Editions du Seuil, 1969).

13. Ibid., p. 158.

14. Julia Kristeva, *Semioteke,* pp. 279-89.

15. Ibid., p. 96.

16. Ibid., pp. 255-77.

17. Michel Serres, *Esthetiques sur Carpaccio* (Paris: Hermann, 1975), one chapter has appeared in translation, "Peter-Stephen Isomorphisms, 2," *Diacritics* (Fall 1975), pp. 39-48.

18. Serres, "Isomorphisms, 2," p. 41.

19. Ibid., p. 43.

20. Ibid.

21. Serres, *Esthetiques sur Carpaccio,* p. 118.

22. Ibid., p. 122.

23. Ibid.

24. Jean-François Lyotard, *Des Dispositifs Pulsionnels* (Paris: 10/18, 1973).

25. Lyotard, *Dérive à partir de Marx et Freud* (Paris: 10/18, 1973).

26. Ibid., p. 55.

27. Lyotard, *Discours, Figures* (Paris: Klinksieck, 1971), p. 225.

28. Lyotard, *Des Dispositifs Pulsionnels,* pp. 95-104.

29. Anton Ehrenzweig, *The Psychoanalysis of Artistic Vision and Hearing* (London: Sheldon, 1965), pp. 22-45.

30. James Hogg, *Psychology and the Visual Arts* (Harmondsworth: Penguin, 1969), pp. 63-137.

31. Rudolph Arnheim, *Art and Visual Perception* (New York: Faber and Faber, 1956), and *Towards a Psychology of Art: Collected Essays, 1967, Visual Thinking* (Berkeley and Los Angeles: University of California Press, 1969).

32. Arnheim, *Film* (London: Faber and Faber, 1933).

33. Lyotard, *Des Dispositifs Pulsionnels,* p. 8.

34. Ibid., p. 9.

35. Jacques Derrida, *L'Ecriture et la Différence* (Paris: Editions du Seuil, 1967), pp. 9-49.

36. Christian Metz, "Le Signifier Imaginaire," and Jean-Louis Baudry, "Le Dispositif," *Communications,* no. 23 (1975).

37. Jacques Lacan, *Les quatres concepts fondamentaux de la psychanalyze* (Paris: Editions du Seuil, 1975), p. 102.

38. Thierry Kuntzel, "Le Défilement," *Cinéma, Théorie, Lectures* (Paris: Klinksieck, 1973), and "Le travail du film, II," *Communications,* no. 23 (1975).

39. Kuntzel, "Le travail du film."

40. Kuntzel, "Le Défilement."

41. Ibid., p. 108.

42. Jacques Lacan, "L'insistence de la lettre dans l'inconscient," *Ecrits* (Paris: Editions du Seuil, 1966) trans. as "The Insistence of the Letter in the Unconscious," *Yale French Studies,* nos. 36-37 (1966), pp. 112-47.

43. "Metamorphosis" as an alternative to the term metaphor is suggested by Lyotard in *Discours, Figures.*

44. Lyotard, *Des Dispositifs,* pp. 53-70.

Chapter 3

1. This is not to say that Brakhage was the first to utilize silence. Hans Richter and Viking Eggling, for example, working in the teens and twenties were concerned with temporal composition within the image track, a theory infused with terminology and concepts borrowed from music theory. While many of their films bear musical titles, *Symphonie Diagonale, Rhythmus, 21, 23* and *25,* and *Fugue,* the presence of visual "orchestration" was to be appreciated to the exclusion of musical accompaniment. In discussing Brakhage I am neither concerned with origins or direct influence, but rather with the growth of a theoretical tendency within the current avant-garde, to which Brakhage contributed both verbally and by the force of his prolific and widely seen filmic statements.

2. As quoted in Sitney, *Visionary Film,* pp. 201-202.

3. Kurt London, *Film Music* (London: Faber and Faber, 1936), p. 27.

4. John Cage, *Silence* (Middletown, Connecticut: Wesleyan University Press, 1961).

5. London, p. 27.

6. Claude Bailblé, Michel Marie, Marie-Claire Ropars, *Muriel* (Paris: Editions Galilée, 1974), p. 85.

7. Ibid., p. 75.

8. Ibid., p. 79.

9. Ibid., p. 85.

10. Henri Pousseur, "The Question of Order in the New Music," in *Perspectives on Contemporary Music Theory,* ed. by Boretz and Cone (New York: W.W. Norton, 1972), p. 110.

11. Ibid., p. 107.

12. Leonard Meyer, *Music, the Arts and Ideas* (Chicago: University of Chicago Press, 1967).

13. Nicholas Ruwet, *Langage, musique, poésie* (Paris: Editions du Seuil, 1972), p. 24.

14. Ibid., p. 30.

15. Pousseur, p. 114.

16. Pousseur, *Fragments Theoriques I sur la musique expérimentale* (Brussels: Editions de l'Institute de Sociologie, 1970), pp. 81-85.

17. Ruwet, p. 26.

18. As cited by Ruwet, p. 26.

19. Cage, p. 68.

20. Ibid., p. 69.

21. Theodor Adorno, *Philosophy of Modern Music*, trans. Anne Mitchell and Wesley Blomster (New York: Seabury Press, 1973).

22. Jean-François Lyotard, *Des dispositifs pulsionnels* (Paris: 10/18, 1973), pp. 115-33.

23. Iwanka Stoianova, "L'énoncé musical," *Musique en Jeu*, no. 19 (June 1975), pp. 21-59.

24. Jean-François Lyotard, *Dérive partir de Marx et Freud* (Paris: 10/18, 1973), pp. 248-71.

25. Michael Nyman, *Experimental Music* (London: Studio Vista, 1974), p. 134.

26. As discussed by Henri Pousseur in *Fragments Theoriques sur la musique expérimentale*, pp. 138-57.

27. Milton Babbitt, "Twelve Tone Rhythmic Structure and the Electronic Medium," in *Perspectives on Contemporary Music Theory*, pp. 149-50.

28. Nyman, p. 124.

Chapter 4

1. *Marcel Duchamp*, ed. Anne d'Harnoncourt and Kynaston McShine (New York: Museum of Modern Art, 1973), p. 146.

2. Lazlo Moholy-Nagy, "Light Architecture," *Industrial Arts*, 1, no. 1 (London, Spring, 1936), reprinted in *Moholy-Nagy*, ed. Richard Kostelanetz (New York: Praeger, 1970), p. 155.

3. Jean-François Lyotard, *Des Dispositifs Pulsionnels* (Paris: 10/18, 1973), especially pp. 237-80, "La Peinture comme dispositif pulsionnel."

4. See Jacob Beck, *Surface, Color, Perception* (Ithaca: Cornell University Press, 1972) for further explanation of these phenomena.

5. James Hogg, *Psychology and the Visual Arts* (Harmondsworth: Penguin, 1969), pp. 65-66.

6. Robert M. Henderson, *D.W. Griffith, The Years at Biograph* (New York: Farrar, Straus, and Giroux, 1970), p. 55.

7. Barry Gerson, "Program Notes: Anthology Film Archives," February 1976.

8. Sigmund Freud, *New Introductory Lectures on Psychoanalysis*, trans. James Strachey (New York: W.W. Norton, 1965), pp. 31-56. See the lecture on "Dreams and Occultism."

9. See, for example, Peter Gidal, "Technology in/through/and Avant-Garde Film: An Instance," a paper for the Milwaukee 20th Century Studies Conference on the Cinematic Apparatus, Technology as Historical and Ideological Form (February 1978).

10. Freud, *Beyond the Pleasure Principle*, trans. James Strachey (New York: Bantam, 1969).

11. Larry Gottheim, "Program Notes: Anthology Film Archives," December 1976.

12. Ibid. McDonald cited on *Blues*.

13. Robert Fleiss, *Erogeneity and Libido* (New York: International Universities Press, 1956), p. 103.

14.   Freud, "'Civilized' Sexual Morality and Modern Nervous Illness," *Standard Edition of the Complete Psychological Works of Sigmund Freud,* vol. 9, p. 187.

15.   Gottheim. Morgan Fisher cited on *Barn Rushes.*

Chapter 5

1.   Jean-François Lyotard, *Des Dispositifs Pulsionnels* (Paris: 10/18, 1973), pp. 53-68.

2.   Sigmund Freud, *Beyond the Pleasure Principle,* trans. James Strachey (New York: Bantam, 1969).

3.   Here I am citing a lecture given by Hollis Frampton at the University of Wisconsin-Madison in 1975.

4.   Georges Bataille, *l'Erotisme* (Paris: Editions du Minuit, 1957), pp. 51-54.

5.   Sigmund Freud, *Totem and Taboo* (New York: Vintage, 1918).

6.   Bataille, pp. 51-54.

7.   Roland Barthes, *S/Z,* trans. Richard Miller (New York: Hill and Wang, 1974), pp. 4-5.

8.   See Jean-François Lyotard's *Dérive à Partir de Marx et Freud* (Paris: 10/18, 1973) and Jean Baudrillard, *The Mirror of Production* (St. Louis: Telos Press, 1975).

9.   S. M. Eisenstein, V. I. Pudovkin and G. V. Alexandrov, "A Statement on the Sound Film" in *Film Form* by Sergei Eisenstein, trans. Jay Leyda (New York: Harcourt, Brace, World, 1949), pp. 257-59.

10.   *Six Years: The Dematerialization of the Art Object,* ed. Lucy Lippard (New York: Praeger, 1973).

11.   Ibid., p. 137.

12.   Wanda Bershin, *"Zorns Lemma," Artforum,* 10, no. 1 (September 1971), p. 44.

13.   Mark Segal, "Hollis Frampton's *Zorns Lemma," Film Culture,* no. 52 (Spring 1971), p. 89.

14.   Bershin, pp. 44-45.

15.   Ibid., p. 45.

16.   Michel Foucault, "Ceçi n'est pas une pipe," *October* (Spring 1976), pp. 7-22.

17.   Ibid., p. 17.

18.   Ibid., p. 12.

Chapter 6

1.   William H. Miller, Floyd Ratliff and H.K. Hartline, "How Cells Receive Stimuli," in *Perception: Mechanisms and Models,* readings from *Scientific American* (San Francisco: W.H. Freeman, 1972), p. 134.

2.   P. Adams Sitney, *Visionary Film* (New York: Oxford University Press, 1974), p. 337.

3.   Ibid., p. 134.

4.   D. H. Hubel, "The Visual Cortex of the Brain," in *Perception: Mechanisms and Models,* (San Francisco: W.H. Freeman, 1972), p. 148.

5. D.H. Hubel, "Introduction: Physiological Analyzers," in *Perception: Mechanisms and Models,* (San Francisco: W.H. Freeman, 1972), p. 148.

6. Tony Conrad, "On *The Flicker,*" in *Experimental Animation* (New York: Van Nostrand Reinhold, 1976), p. 152.

7. Joseph Anderson and Edward Small, "What's in a Flicker Film?" *Communication Monographs,* 43, no. 1 (March 1976).

8. Ibid., p. 31.

9. Ibid., p. 32.

10. Ibid.

11. Both Cornwell and Sitney mention this reformulation of phonemes, as does Paul S. Arthur in his contribution to *A History of the American Avant-Garde Cinema* (New York: The American Federation of Arts, 1976), p. 141. None of these writers explores the theoretical implications of this response, however.

12. Lacan uses imaginary to refer to the domain of images conscious or unconscious, perceived or imagined, whereas symbolic is the order of signifiers which determine the subject. See Jacques Lacan, *Ecrits,* trans. Alan Sheridan (New York: W.W. Norton, 1977).

13. Anton Ehrenzweig, *The Hidden Order of Art* (Berkeley: University of California Press, 1967), p. 3.

14. Sitney, p. 427.

Chapter 7

1. Michel Foucault, *The Order of Things* (New York: Vintage, 1976).

2. Ibid., p. 16.

3. Pierre Francastel, *La Figure et le lieu* (Paris: Gallimard, 1967), p. 69.

4. Rowland Mainstone, "Intuition and the Springs of Structural Invention," in *Structures, Implicit and Explicit,* ed. James Bryan and Rolf Sauer (Philadelphia: Falcon, 1973), p. 48.

5. Arnold Hauser, *The Social History of Art,* vol. 2 (New York: Vintage, 1951), p. 28.

6. Stephen Heath, "Narrative Space," *Screen,* 17, no. 3 (Autumn 1976).

7. Jonas Mekas, "Ernie Gehr Interviewed on March 24, 1971," *Film Cultures,* nos. 53, 54, 55 (Spring 1971), p. 25.

8. "Letter from Michel Snow," *Film Culture,* no. 46 (Autumn 1967), p. 4.

9. Christian Norberg-Schulz, *Existence, Space and Architecture* (New York: Praeger, 1971), p. 91.

10. Ibid.

11. As quoted by Carla Gottlieb in *Beyond Modern Art* (New York: Dutton, 1976), p. 237.

12. Dore O., "Program Notes," Anthology Film Archives, Dec. 11-13, 1975.

13. Anton Ehrenzweig, *The Hidden Order of Art* (Berkeley: University of California Press, 1967).

14. John Berger, *Ways of Seeing* (New York, Viking, 1973), p. 105.

14. Serafina Bathrick, "The Past is Future: Family and the American Home and *Meet Me in St. Louis,*" *The Minnesota Review,* NS (Spring 1976), pp. 132-39.

15. Larry Gottheim, "Program Notes," Anthology Film Archives, Dec. 2-4, 1976.

16. Ibid.

17. Ehrenzweig, *The Psychoanalysis of Artistic Seeing and Hearing* (London: Sheldon, 1965), pp. 196-96.

18. Ibid., p. 18.

19. Jean-François Lyotard, *Des Dispositifs Pulsionnels* (Paris: 10/18, 1976), p. 86.

20. Ibid., p. 88.

21. Werner Nekes, "Program Notes," Anthology Film Archives, Dec. 11-13, 1975.

22. Ibid.

23. Ehrenzweig, *The Psychoanalysis of Artistic Seeing and Hearing,* pp. 109-11.

24. Lyotard, "The Unconscious as Mise-en-scène," *Performance* in *Post-Modern Culture,* trans. Joseph Meyer, Madison, Wisconsin, Coda Press: 1977, pp. 87-98.

25. Michael Snow, "On *La Région Centrale,*" *Film Culture,* no. 5 (Spring 1971), p. 58.

26. Ibid.

Selected Bibliography

Adorno, Theodor. *Philosophy of Modern Music.* Trans. Anne Mitchell and Wesley Blomster. New York: Seabury, 1973.

Afterimage. Special Issue. "Perspectives on English Independent Cinema," no. 6 (Summer 1976).

Artforum. Special Film Issue. 10, no. 1 (September 1971).

_____. "Eisenstein/Brakhage." 11, no. 5 (January 1973).

Arnheim, Rudolf. *Art and Visual Perception.* New York: Farber and Farber, 1956.

_____. *Film.* London: Farber and Farber, 1963.

_____. *Towards a Psychology of Art: Collected Essays.* Berkeley: University of California Press, 1967.

_____. *Visual Thinking.* Berkeley: University of California Press, 1969.

Baible, Claude, Michel Marie and Marie-Claire Ropars. *Muriel.* Paris: Editions Galilee, 1974.

Barthes, Roland. *S/Z.* Paris: Editions du Seuil, 1970. Trans. Richard Miller. New York: Hill and Wang, 1974.

_____. "Le Troisième Sens." *Cahiers du Cinéma,* no. 222 (juillet 1970). Trans. as "The Third Meaning" in *Artforum,* 11, no. 5 (January 1973).

_____. "Le Message Photographique." *Communications,* no. 1 (1962).

_____. "Rhetorique de l'image." *Communications,* no. 4 (1964).

Bataille, Georges. *L'Erotisme.* Paris: Editions du Minuit, 1957. Trans. as *Eroticism* by Mary Dalwood. London: Calder, 1962.

Battock, Gregory, ed. *The New American Cinema.* New York: Dutton, 1967.

_____. ed. *The New Art.* New York: Dutton, 1967.

Baudry, Jean-Pierre. "Cinéma: éffets ideologique produit par l'appareil de base." *Cinéthique,* nos. 7-8: 1-8. Trans. as "Ideological Effects of the Basic Apparatus." Alan Williams. *Film Quarterly* 28, no. 2 (Winter 1974): 39-47.

_____. "Le Dispositif." *Communications,* no. 23 (1976). Trans. as "The Apparatus." *Camera Obscura,* no. 1. (1977): 104-28.

Beck, Jacob. *Surface, Color, Perception.* Ithaca: Cornell University Press, 1972.

Benjamin, Walter. *Illuminations.* Trans. Harry Zohn. New York: Schocken, 1969.

Berger, John. *Ways of Seeing.* New York: Viking, 1973.

Bershin, Wanda. "*Zorns Lemma.*" *Artforum,* 10, no. 1 (September 1971): 41-45.

Brakhage, Stan. "Metaphors on vision." *Film Culture,* no. 30. (Autumn 1963).

Boretz, Benjamin and Cone, Edward, eds. *Perspectives on Contemporary Music Theory,* New York: W.W. Norton, 1972.

Cage, John. *Silence.* Middletown, Conn.: Weslyan University Press, 1961.

Comiolli, Jean Louis. "Technique et idéologie," *Cahiers du Cinéma,* nos. 229, 230, 231, 233, 234-35 (1971-72).

Cornwell, Regina. "Ten Years of Snow." Evanston: Northwestern University, 1975.

———. "Illusion and Object." *Artforum* 10, no. 1 (September 1971): 56-62.

———. "Some Formalist Tendencies in the Current Avant-Garde Film." *Kansas Quarterly* 4, no. 2 (Spring 1972): 60-70.

Curtis, David. *Experimental Cinema.* New York: Delta, 1971.

Derrida, Jacques. *L'Ecriture et la difference.* Paris: Editions du Seuil, 1967.

———. *Of Grammatology.* Trans. Gayatri Spivak. Baltimore: Johns Hopkins University Press, 1974.

Ehrenzweig, Anton. *The Hidden Order of Art.* Berkeley: University of California Press, 1967.

———. *The Psychoanalysis of Artistic Seeing and Hearing.* London: Sheldon, 1965.

Eco, Umberto. *La Structure Absente.* Paris: Mercure de France, 1972.

Eisenstein, Sergei. *Film Form.* Trans. Jay Leyda. New York: Harcourt, Brace, World, 1949.

———. *Film Sense.* Trans. Jay Leyda. New York: Harcourt, Brace, World, 1942.

Foucault, Michel. *Les Mots et Les Choses.* Paris: Gallimard, 1966. Trans. as *The Order of Things.* New York: Vintage, 1976.

———. "Ceci n'est pas une pipe." *October* (Spring 1976):7-22.

Francastel, Pierre. *Le Figure et le lieu.* Paris: Gallimard, 1967.

Freud, Sigmund. *Beyond the Pleasure Principle.* Trans. James Strachey. New York: Bantam, 1969.

———. *The Ego and the Id.* Trans. Joan Riviere. New York: Norton, 1960.

———. *Group Psychology and the Analysis of the Ego.* Trans. James Strachey. New York: Bantam, 1960.

———. *Interpretation of Dreams.* Trans. James Strachey. New York: Norton, 1965.

———. *An Outline of Psychoanalysis.* Trans. James Strachey. New York: Norton, 1969.

———. *Three Case Histories.* Trans. Philip Rieff. New York: Collier, 1963.

———. *Totem and Taboo.* Trans. A.A. Brill. New York: Vintage, 1918.

Gerritson, Frans. *Theory and Practice of Color.* New York: Van Nostrand, Reinhold, 1975.

Gerson, Barry. "Program Notes: Anthology Film Archives." (1976).

Gidal, Peter, ed. *Structural Film Anthology.* London: British Film Institute, 1976.

———. "Technology in/through/and Avant-Garde Film" Milwaukee, 1976. Paper delivered at a Conference sponsored by the Center for Twentieth Century Studies. University of Wisconsin, Milwaukee.

Godfrid, E. and Rabinovitch, G.H. "Werner Nekes: Notes sur T.WO.MEN." *Ça* 3, no. 9 (1976):58-67.

Gottheim, Larry. "Program Notes: Anthology Film Archives," New York, 1976.

Gottlieb, Carla. *Beyond Modern Art.* New York: Dutton, 1976.

Hauser, Arnold. *The Social History of Art.* Vol. 2. New York: Vintage, 1951.

Heath, Stephen. "Narrative Space," *Screen* 17, no. 3 (Autumn, 1975).

———. "On Screen, in frame: Film and Ideology." *Quarterly Review of Film Studies* 1, no. 3 (August 1976):251-65.

Held, Richard and Whitman, Richards, eds. *Perception: Mechanisms and Models.* San Francisco: W.H. Freeman, 1972.

Henderson, Robert. *D.W. Griffith: The Years at Biograph.* New York: Farrar, Straus and Giroux, 1970.

Hogg, James. *Psychology and the Visual Arts.* Harmondsworth: Penguin, 1969.

Kostelanetz, Richard. *Moholy-Nagy.* New York: Praeger, 1970.

Kozloff, Max. "The Authoritarian Personality in Modern Art." *Artforum* 12, no. 9. (May 1974):40-48.

Krauss, Rosalind. "Paul Sharits: Stop time." *Artforum* 11, no. 8. (April 1973):60-61.

Kristeva, Julia. *Polylogues*. Paris: Editions du Seuil, 1977.

_____. *La Révolution du langage poétique*. Paris: Editions du Seuil, 1975.

_____. *Semiotike: Recherches pour une sémanalyse*. Paris: Editions du Seuil, 1969.

_____. "Cinéma, Pratique analytique, Pratique Révolutionaire." *Cinéthique*, no. 9-10:71-79.

_____. "Ellipse sur la frayeur et la seduction spéculaire." *Communications*, no. 23 (1976).

_____. "The Semiotic Activity." *Screen*, no. 2 (1973):23-39.

Kuntzel, Thierry. "Le travail du film." *Communications*, no. 19 (1972):25-40.

_____. "Le travail du film II." *Communications*, no. 23 (1976).

_____. "Savoir, Pouvoir, Voir." *Ça*. 2, no. 7/8 (mai 1975):85-97.

Lacan, Jacques. *Ecrits* I et II. Paris: Editions du Seuil, 1966. Trans. as *Ecrits*. New York: Norton, 1977.

_____. *Les Quatre Concepts Fondamentaux de la psychanalyze*. Paris: Editions du Seuil, 1975.

Locke, John W. "Michael Snow's *La Region Centrale*." *Artforum* 12, no. 3:66-71 and no. 4:66-72.

_____. "Standish Lawder." *Artforum* 12, no. 9 (May 1974):50-54.

Lippard, Lucy, ed. *Six Years: The Dematerialization of the Art Object*. New York: Praeger, 1973.

London, Kurt. *Film Music*. London: Faber and Faber, 1936.

Lyotard, Jean-François. *Des Dispositifs Pulsionnels*. Paris: 10/18, 1973.

_____. *Dérive à partir de Marx et Freud*. Paris: 10/18, 1973.

_____. *Discours, Figures*. Paris: Klinksieck, 1971.

_____. *Economie Libidinal*. Paris: Les Editions du Minuit, 1974.

_____. "The Unconscious as Mise-en-scène," *Performances in Post-Modern Culture*. Trans. Joseph Meyer. Madison, Wisconsin: Coda Press, 1977, pp. 87-98.

Mekas, Jonas. *Movie Journal*. New York: Collier Books, 1972.

_____. "Ernie Gehr Interviewed on March 24, 1971," *Film Culture*, nos. 53, 54, 55 (Spring 1971).

Metz, Christian. *Essais sur la signification au cinéma*. 2 vols. Paris: Klinksieck, 1968 and 1972. Trans. as *Film Language*.

_____. *Langage et Cinéma*. Paris: Klinksieck, 1971. Trans. as *Language and Cinema*. The Hague: Mouton, 1974.

_____. "Le Signifiant imaginaire," *Communications*, no. 23 (1976):3-55. Trans. as "The Imaginary Signifier." *Screen* 16, no. 2 (Summer 1975):14-76.

Meyer, Leonard B. *Music, the Arts, and Ideas*. Chicago: University of Chicago Press, 1967.

Michelson, Annette. "Book review of Bazin's *What is Cinema*." *Artforum* 6, no. 10 (Summer 1968):67-71.

_____. "Film and the Radical Aspiration." *Film Culture*, no. 42 (Fall 1966):34-43, 136.

_____. "Paul Sharits and the Critique of Illusionism: An Introduction." Minneapolis: Walker Art Center, 1974.

_____. "Toward Snow." *Artforum* 9, no. 10 (June 1971):30-37.

Mitry, Jean. *Cinéma Expérimentale*. Paris: Editions Seghers, 1971.

Moles, Abraham. *Les Musiques expérimentales*. Paris: Editions du Cercle d'art contemporain, 1960.

Mulvey, Laura. "Visual Pleasure and Narrative Cinema." *Screen* 16, no. 3 (Autumn 1975):6-18.

Nekes, Werner. "Program Notes: Anthology Film Archives." New York (December 1975).

Norberg-Schulz, Christian. *Existence, Space and Architecture*. New York: Praeger, 1971.

Nyman, Michael. *Experimental Music*. London: Studio Vista, 1974.

O., Dore. "Program Notes: Anthology Film Archives." (December 1975).

Padgham, C.A. and J.E. Saunders. *The Perception of Light and Color*. New York: Academic Press, 1975.

Poggioli, Renato. *Theory of the Avant-Garde*. Trans. Gerald Fitzgerald. Cambridge: Belnap Press, 1968.

Pousseur, Henri. *Fragments Théoriques I sur la musique expérimentale.* Bruxelles: Editions de L'Institute, de Sociologie, 1970.

_____. *Musique, Semantic, Société.* Paris: Casterman, 1972.

Renan, Sheldon. *An Introduction to the American Underground Film.* New York: Dutton, 1967.

Rothchild, Edward. *The Meaning of Unintelligibility in Modern Art.* New York: Oriole, 1934.

Russett, Robert and Cecile Starr, eds. *Experimental Animation.* New York: Van Nostrand and Reinhold, 1976.

Saunders, J.E. and Padgham, C.A. *The Perception of Light and Color.* New York: Academic Press, 1975.

Schefer, Jean-Louis. *Scenographie d'un tableau.* Paris: Editions du Seuil, 1969.

_____. "Les Couleurs renversees/la buée" *Cahiers du Cinéma,* no. 230 (juillet 1971):28-42.

_____. "En marge d'une semiologie de l'image." *Ça.* 2, no. 7/8 (mai 1975):52-58.

Schorr, Justin. *Toward the Transformation of Art.* Cranbury, N.J.: Associated University Presses, 1974.

Segel, Mark. "Hollis Frampton's *Zorns Lemma*" *Film Culture,* no. 52 (Spring 1971):88-94.

Serres, Michel. *Esthetiques sur Carpaccio.* Paris: Hermann, 1975.

_____. "Peter-Stephen Isomorphisms 2." *Diacritics* (Fall 1975):39-48.

Sitney, P. Adams, ed. *Film Culture Reader.* New York: Praeger: 1970.

_____. *Visionary Film.* New York: Oxford University Press, 1974.

_____. "The Idea of Morphology," *Film Culture,* nos. 53, 54, 55 (Spring 1971).

Snow, Michael. *Cover to Cover.* The Presses of the Nova Scotia College of Art and Design and New York University, 1977.

_____. *A Survey.* Ontario: Art Gallery of Ontario, 1970.

_____. "On *La Région Centrale.*" *Film Culture,* no. 52 (Spring 1970):58.

Stoianova, Iwanka. "L'Enoncé Musicale" *Musique en Jeu,* no. 19 (June 1975):21-57.

Studio International. Special Issue. "Architecture ◄——►Art." 190, no. 977 (Sept./Oct. 1975).

_____. Special Issue. "Art and Photography." 190, No. 976 (July/August 1975).

_____. Special Issue. "Avant-Garde Film in England and Europe." 190, no. 978 (Nov./Dec. 1975).

Trytall, Gilbert. *Principles and Practice of Electronic Music.* New York: Grosset and Dunlap, 1973.

Tyler, Parker. *Underground Film—A Critical History.* New York: Grove Press, 1969.

Wollen, Peter. "Ontology and Materialism in Film." *Screen* 17, no. 1 (Spring 1975):7-23.

Youngblood, Gene. *Expanded Cinema.* New York: Dutton, 1970.

Index

Adorno, Theodore, 39-40
Alpha Mondala, 99
Analogy, 9
Anaphoric function, 12, 17
Anderson, Joseph, 99
  Alpha Mondala
Architecture, 6, 107-22
Arnheim, Rudolf, 18, 19
Art and Visual Perception, 19
Autumnal Equinox, 77-79
Avant-Garde
  definition, 4, 5, 6
  sound track, 35-49
Axiomatic Granularity, 21
  (Back and Forth), 113-21

Barn Rushes, 64, 70-71
Barry, Gene
  "Note: Make a Painting of a Note as a
    Painting", 85
Barthes, Roland, 2, 7, 8, 9, 10, 11
  writerly text, 77
Bataille, Georges, 76
*The Battle of Tokyo of the Story of a Young
  Man Who Left His Will on Film*, 131
Baudelaire, 13
Baudrillard, Jean, 79
Baudry, Jean-Louis, 9, 10, 21
Bazin, André, 7
Berger, John, 121
Bershin, Wanda, 89
Bitzer, Billy
  use of iris mattes, 57
Blazes, 46-47
Blues, 65-68, 93
Bordone, Paris, 10
Brakhage, Stan, 1, 29-30, 94-96
  Dog-Star Man, 82
  Scenes from Under Childhood, 82
  Troegoedia, 77
  Window Water Baby Moving, 82
  The Wonder Ring, 56

Bresson, Robert, 4
Burch, Noel, 3

Cage, John, 41
  In Between, 29
  Silence, 31
Cartesian Meditations, 123
Cézanne, Paul, 16, 20, 124-25
Classical film, 3
Codes, 2, 4, 8, 9, 27
Cognitive psychology, 55
Color
  experiments in perception, 55
  modes of appearance, illumination and
    surface, 55
Color Sound Frames, 100
Computer-generated images, 43
Conceptual film, 83-91
Conrad, Tony
  The Flicker, 96-99
Corn, 65, 68-69
Critical Mass, 44-46, 90, 93
Crossroads, 47-48

Deconstruction, 1
Denotation, 7, 8
Deren, Maya, 1
Derrida, Jacques, 1, 21
Diegetic sound, 32
Disjunction, 43
Dispositifs, 53
Duchamp, Marcel, 52-53
Duras, Marguerite, 34-35
Duvivier, Jacques
  Pepe Le Moko, 32

Eco, Umberto, 8, 9
Ecriture, 12
Ehrenzweig, Anton, 18, 19, 124, 127
Electro-acoustic composition, 42
l'Emouvior, 24
Empire, 64

Endurance/Remembrance/Metamorphosis, 54, 64
Eroticism, 76
Esthetiques Sur Carpaccio, 14
Existence, Space and Architecture, 117
Expression, 17

Figural, 17
Filmic writing, 2
Fire of Waters, 30
Flavin, Don
    light sculptures, 119
Fleiss, Robert
    psychoanalytic view of eye-mouth unit, 67-68
Flicker, 6, 93-105
The Flicker, 96-99
Fog Line, 64-65, 122
Force, 18, 21
Foucault, Michel, 90-91
    The Order of Things, 107-8
Frampton, Hollis, 30
    Autumnal Equinox, 26, 77-79
    Critical Mass, 44-46, 90, 93
    Lemon, 22-27
    "The Magellan Cycle", 73-76
    Nostalgia, 85-86
    Poetic Justice, 83-86
    Procession, 80
    Summer Solstice, 77-79
    Surface Tension, 91
    The Gates of Death, 75-78
    Winter Solstice, 77-79
    Zorns Lemma, 86-91
Francastal, Pierre, 108
Freud, Sigmund, 16, 17, 18, 21
    Beyond the Pleasure Principle, 63, 73
"Freud Salon Cézanne", 16

The Gates of Death, 78
Gehr, Ernie
    Axiomatic Granularity, 21
    Serene Velocity, 110-111
    Wait, 112-13
Geno-text, 12
Gerson, Barry, 30, 52, 94
    Endurance/Rememberance/
        Metamorphosis, 25-26, 54-58, 64
    Luminous Zone, 60-63
    paracinematic sculpture, 52-53
    Translucent Appearances, 58-60, 63
Gestalt psychology, 18, 19
    pattern perception, 37-38
Gordon, Bette
    Still-Life, 77
Gottheim, Larry, 30, 52
    Barn Rushes, 64, 70-71, 122

Blues, 65-68, 93
Corn, 65, 68-69
Fog Line, 64-65
Harmonica, 70-72
Horizons, 122-24
Mouches Volantes, 80-83
Griffith, D.W.
    use of iris mattes, 57

Harmonica, 70-72
Hauser, Arnold, 109, 121
Hermann, Bernard
    scores for Hitchcock's films, 33
Hermaneutic codes, 2
Horizons, 122-24

Iconography, 7
Iconology, 7
Image, 6
    monocular, 10
    photographic, 7
    referentiality, 73-76
    Renaissance, 10, 16
India Song, 35
Interim, 29
Intertextuality, 13

Jean-Luc Godard, 34
La Jetée, 85

King Kong, 109
Kristeva, Julia, 2, 11, 12, 13, 16, 38-40
Kubelka, Peter, 5
    Schwechater, 95-96
Kuntzel, Thierry, 24
    "Le Defilement", 24, 25

La Rouchefoucauld, 13
Lacan, Jacques, 53
Landscape, 6, 121-31
Lautréament, 13
Lemon, 22-27
Lexia, 11
Libidinal economy, 21
Luminous Zone, 60-63
Lyotard, Jean-François, 16, 17, 18, 19, 20, 21, 26, 39-40, 53, 56, 68, 73, 78-79, 124-5, 128

Mainstone, Rowland, 108-9
Marie, Michel, 33
Marker, Chris, 85
Makimono, 125-126, 129
Mattes, 52, 57-59
McDonald, Scott, 65
Meisel
    music for Potemkin, Berlin, Portrait of a City, 32

Melies, George, 25
Menkin, Marie, 1
Metz, Christian, 2, 3, 4, 9, 21
Meyer, Leonard, 38
Minimalism, 43, 51
Modernist film, 4, 69-70
    sound track, 33
Moholy-nagy, Lazlo, 52, 53
Moore, Anthony, 126
Mouches Volantes, 80-83
Muriel, 33-34
Music, the Arts and Ideas, 38

N:O:T:H:I:N:G, 101-3
Nekes, Werner, 5
    Makimono, 125-26, 129
Nondiegetic sound tracks, 32
Norberg-Schulz, Christian, 117
Nostalgia, 85-86

O., Dore, 5
    Kaskara, 120-121
Ontology of cinema, 1
Oshima, Nagisa, 131

Paik, Nam June
    Tribute to John Cage, 31
Paracinematic sculpture, 52-53
Paradigm, 11, 13
Paradigmatic oppositions, 77
Pascal, Blaise, 13
Pepe Le Moko, 32
Poetic Justice, 83-86
Posseur, Henri, 37-38, 41
Process music, 37-39
Procession, 80
Psychoperceptual theory, 55, 97-98
Pyrotechnics, 78-79

Ray Gun Virus, 100-101
Reich, Steve, 41, 44
La Région Central, 125, 128-29
Repetition, 43, 51, 75
Resnais, Alain, 33-34
Reversibility, 76-77
Rivette, Jacques, 34
Robbe-Grillet, Alain, 34
    La Jalousie, l'Imortelle, 59
Rochas, Glauber, 34
Ruwet, Nicholas, 38, 41

S/Z, 11
Satie, Erik
    music for *Entr'acte*, 32
Schefer, Jean-Louis, 10, 11, 14, 21
Schwechater, 95-96

Scopophilia, 67-68
Segal, Mark, 88
Semiotics, 21
    of image, 7-27
    of sound, 32-49
Serene Velocity, 110-11
serial music, 37-39
Serres, Michel, 10, 21, 79, 108
Sharits, Paul, 99
    Color Sound Frames, 100
    N:O:T:H:I:N:G, 101, 103
    Ray Gun Virus, 100
    T, O, U, C, H, I, N, G, 101-5
Signifiance, 12, 13, 16, 40, 89
Small, Edward
    Alpha Mandala, 99
Snow, Michael, 5
    (Back and Forth), 113-121
    La Region Centrale, 125, 128-9
    Wavelength, 35
Son Nom de Venise en Calcutta Desert, 35
Sound, 6
Sound track
    avant-garde, 35-49
    modernist, 32-35
Still-Life, 77
Stockhausen, Karlhans, 42
Stoinova, Iwanka, 40, 49
Summer Solstice, 77-79
Surface Tension, 91
Suture, 3
Syntagma, 11, 13

T, O, U, C, H, I, N, G, 101-5
Tenney, Jim, 29
Textual systems, 2, 4
Theory of Film Practice, 3
Translucent Appearances, 58-60, 63
Troegoedia, 77
trompe l'oeil, 27
Two or Three Things I Know About Her, 34

Une Partie d'echecs, 10

Visionary Film, 96

Wait, 112-13
Warhol, Andy
    Empire, 64
Wavelength, 112-17
Ways of Seeing, 121
Winter Solstice, 77-79
Women filmmakers, 5
The Wonder Ring, 56

Zorns Lemma, 86-91